Modern Critical Interpretations

William Shakespeare's
The Winter's Tale

Modern Critical Interpretations

The Oresteia
Beowulf
The General Prologue to
  The Canterbury Tales
The Pardoner's Tale
The Knight's Tale
The Divine Comedy
Exodus
Genesis
The Gospels
The Iliad
The Book of Job
Volpone
Doctor Faustus
The Revelation of St.
  John the Divine
The Song of Songs
Oedipus Rex
The Aeneid
The Duchess of Malfi
Antony and Cleopatra
As You Like It
Coriolanus
Hamlet
Henry IV, Part I
Henry IV, Part II
Henry V
Julius Caesar
King Lear
Macbeth
Measure for Measure
The Merchant of Venice
A Midsummer Night's
  Dream
Much Ado About
  Nothing
Othello
Richard II
Richard III
The Sonnets
Taming of the Shrew
The Tempest
Twelfth Night
The Winter's Tale
Emma
Mansfield Park
Pride and Prejudice
The Life of Samuel
  Johnson
Moll Flanders
Robinson Crusoe
Tom Jones
The Beggar's Opera
Gray's Elegy
Paradise Lost
The Rape of the Lock
Tristram Shandy
Gulliver's Travels

Evelina
The Marriage of Heaven
  and Hell
Songs of Innocence and
  Experience
Jane Eyre
Wuthering Heights
Don Juan
The Rime of the Ancient
  Mariner
Bleak House
David Copperfield
Hard Times
A Tale of Two Cities
Middlemarch
The Mill on the Floss
Jude the Obscure
The Mayor of
  Casterbridge
The Return of the Native
Tess of the D'Urbervilles
The Odes of Keats
Frankenstein
Vanity Fair
Barchester Towers
The Prelude
The Red Badge of
  Courage
The Scarlet Letter
The Ambassadors
Daisy Miller, The Turn
  of the Screw, and
  Other Tales
The Portrait of a Lady
Billy Budd, Benito Cer-
  eno, Bartleby the Scriv-
  ener, and Other Tales
Moby-Dick
The Tales of Poe
Walden
Adventures of
  Huckleberry Finn
The Life of Frederick
  Douglass
Heart of Darkness
Lord Jim
Nostromo
A Passage to India
Dubliners
A Portrait of the Artist as
  a Young Man
Ulysses
Kim
The Rainbow
Sons and Lovers
Women in Love
1984
Major Barbara

Man and Superman
Pygmalion
St. Joan
The Playboy of the
  Western World
The Importance of Being
  Earnest
Mrs. Dalloway
To the Lighthouse
My Antonia
An American Tragedy
Murder in the Cathedral
The Waste Land
Absalom, Absalom!
Light in August
Sanctuary
The Sound and the Fury
The Great Gatsby
A Farewell to Arms
The Sun Also Rises
Arrowsmith
Lolita
The Iceman Cometh
Long Day's Journey Into
  Night
The Grapes of Wrath
Miss Lonelyhearts
The Glass Menagerie
A Streetcar Named
  Desire
Their Eyes Were
  Watching God
Native Son
Waiting for Godot
Herzog
All My Sons
Death of a Salesman
Gravity's Rainbow
All the King's Men
The Left Hand of
  Darkness
The Brothers Karamazov
Crime and Punishment
Madame Bovary
The Interpretation of
  Dreams
The Castle
The Metamorphosis
The Trial
Man's Fate
The Magic Mountain
Montaigne's Essays
Remembrance of Things
  Past
The Red and the Black
Anna Karenina
War and Peace

These and other titles in preparation

William Shakespeare's
The Winter's Tale

Edited and with an introduction by
Harold Bloom
Sterling Professor of the Humanities
Yale University

Chelsea House Publishers ◊ *1987*
NEW YORK ◊ NEW HAVEN ◊ PHILADELPHIA

© 1987 by Chelsea House Publishers,
a division of Chelsea House Educational Communications, Inc.,
95 Madison Avenue, New York, NY 10016
345 Whitney Avenue, New Haven, CT 06511
5014 West Chester Pike, Edgemont, PA 19028

Introduction © 1987 by Harold Bloom

Printed and bound in the United States of America

∞ The paper used in this publication meets the minimum
requirements of the American National Standard for Permanence
of Paper for Printed Library Materials, Z39.48-1984.

Library of Congress Cataloging-in-Publication Data
Shakespeare's The Winter's Tale.
   (Modern critical interpretations)
   Bibliography: p.
   Includes index.
   Summary: A collection of critical essays on
Shakespeare's play "The Winter's Tale" arranged in
chronological order of publication.
   1. Shakespeare, William, 1564–1616.   Winter's tale.
[1. Shakespeare, William, 1564–1616.   Winter's tale.
2. English drama—History and criticism]   I. Bloom,
Harold.   II. Series.
PR2839.W54   1987   822.3′3   86-31021
ISBN 0-87754-942-7 (alk. paper)

Contents

Editor's Note

This book gathers together a representative selection of the best critical essays available upon Shakespeare's late pastoral romance, *The Winter's Tale*. The essays are reprinted here in the chronological order of their original publication. I am grateful to Katherine Treadwell for her devoted labor in helping me to edit this volume.

My introduction contrasts the nihilistic, projective jealousy of Leontes with the value-conferring generosity of Perdita. G. Wilson Knight begins the chronological sequence of criticism with his rather Wordsworthian reading of the play, in which a continuity between past and present is realized anew as an act of healing for the self. In a study of repetition as a mode by which good and evil mutually restrain one another, James Edward Siemon presents the play's earlier and later movements as a dialectic of something rather less than healing.

L. C. Knights, exploring the image of "integration" in *The Winter's Tale*, looks carefully at the question of the relevance of psychoanalytic criticism to the play. In a very positive reading, Carol Thomas Neely commends the play for its healthy sexuality, and for allowing its women a fully human status. Studying tragic structure in this late Shakespearean romance, Charles Frey finds an element he can judge tragic in the drama's effect upon its audience, particularly the hunger it stimulates in them for the "comfort of awakening faith."

Anne Barton considers *The Winter's Tale* as an amalgam of several kinds of fiction, while Louis L. Martz relates the play to the entire Renaissance enterprise of Humanism. In this book's final essay, Richard Studing revises the customary view of the pastoral scene in act 4, finding in it darker elements than "the simplicity, naturalness, and pristine values of Bohemia," in which the pretenses and conflicts of that idealized country are exposed.

Introduction

Winter's tales, then and now, tend to be wild chronicles, fantastic stories told by the fireside. Once accounted a comedy, Shakespeare's *The Winter's Tale* is now considered a romance, together with *Pericles* and *Cymbeline* before it and *The Tempest* beyond it. Granted that the comedy of one era is hardly that of another, it would still be difficult to think of *The Winter's Tale* as a comedy. Yet we think of *Measure for Measure* as a comedy (a "problem play" is not a genre), and there are dark affinities between it and *The Winter's Tale*. In *The Winter's Tale* everything again is beyond absurdity, ranging from a spectacularly unexpected, paranoid jealousy and murderousness to the resurrection of the statue as the living Hermione. The Shakespeare who writes *The Winter's Tale* might almost be Anthony Burgess's Shakespeare in *Nothing like the Sun* and *Enderby's Dark Lady*. This is an overtly outrageous Shakespeare, deliberately provoking to fury his empirical friend and rival, Ben Jonson, by giving Bohemia a sea-coast.

On that spurious coast poor Antigonus exits, pursued by a bear, in a stage direction worthy of Groucho Marx. As with *Measure for Measure*, all that matters is the staging of a fantastic story, an entertainment so designed that it allows for a totally original and most powerful meditation upon death in *Measure for Measure*, and in *The Winter's Tale* allows for the pastoral phantasmagoria of act 4 and for our enchantment by Perdita. Perdita, I will venture, *is* the play, the goddess Flora incarnated in a personality so fresh and winning that reality cannot hold out against her. She is everything in herself, while happily not needing to know it, whereas Leontes moves towards madness because he fears that he is nothing in

1

himself, a fear which he projects upon everyone and everything else:

> Is whispering nothing?
> Is leaning cheek to cheek? is meeting noses?
> Kissing with inside lip? stopping the career
> Of laughter with a sigh (a note infallible
> Of breaking honesty)? horsing foot on foot?
> Skulking in corners? wishing clocks more swift?
> Hours, minutes? noon, midnight? and all eyes
> Blind with the pin and web but theirs, theirs only,
> That would unseen be wicked? Is this nothing?
> Why then the world and all that's in't is nothing,
> The covering sky is nothing, Bohemia nothing,
> My wife is nothing, nor nothing have these nothings,
> If this be nothing.

One dozen rhetorical questions, followed by six assertions of total nihilism, is an astonishing structure for a speech, yet marvelously appropriate for a descent through sudden and wholly irrational jealousy into the death drive. Othello has Iago, but Leontes has nothing:

> Affection! thy intention stabs the centre.
> Thou dost make possible things not so held,
> Communicat'st with dreams (how can this be?),
> With what's unreal thou co-active art,
> And fellow'st nothing. Then 'tis very credent
> Thou mayst co-join with something, and thou dost
> (And that beyond commission), and I find it
> (And that to the infection of my brains
> And hard'ning of my brows).

Hallett Smith, in the very useful *Riverside Shakespeare*, reads "affection" here not as "desire" but as Leontes' own jealousy. Probably both readings are right, since Leontes' projected jealousy is also his own unruly desire, a return of repressed bisexuality, with its deep need for betrayal. Shakespeare's beautiful irony is that "affection" here is meant by Leontes as the sexual drive of the supposed lovers, yet manifestly projects his own murderous jealousy. For a romance to begin with a paranoid siege of jealousy is profoundly appropriate, and demonstrates Shakespeare to be Proust's (and Freud's) largest precursor. *The Winter's Tale*, even as a title, becomes a story of projected jealousy and its antidote, whose name is Perdita.

II

Even Shakespeare has nothing else as ecstatic as act 4 of *The Winter's Tale*, which has established one of the limits of literature as an art. Autolycus is one kind of splendor, setting the context by bold contrast to "an art / Which does mend Nature—change it rather; but / The art itself is Nature." That art is Perdita's nature, and becomes Florizel's:

PER: O Proserpina,
For the flow'rs now, that, frighted, thou let'st fall
From Dis's waggon! daffadils,
That come before the swallow dares, and take
The winds of March with beauty; violets, dim,
But sweeter than the lids of Juno's eyes,
Or Cytherea's breath; pale primeroses,
That die unmarried, ere they can behold
Bright Phoebus in his strength (a malady
Most incident to maids); bold oxlips, and
The crown imperial; lilies of all kinds
(The flow'r-de-luce being one). O, these I lack,
To make you garlands of, and my sweet friend,
To strew him o'er and o'er!
FLO: What? like a corse?
PER: No, like a bank, for love to lie and play on;
Not like a corse; or if—not to be buried,
But quick and in mine arms. Come, take your flow'rs.
Methinks I play as I have seen them do
In Whitsun pastorals. Sure this robe of mine
Does change my disposition.
FLO: What you do
Still betters what is done. When you speak, sweet,
I'ld have you do it ever; when you sing,
I'ld have you buy and sell so; so give alms;

Pray so; and for the ord'ring your affairs,
To sing them too. When you do dance, I wish you
A wave o' th' sea, that you might ever do
Nothing but that; move still, still so,
And own no other function. Each your doing
(So singular in each particular)
Crowns what you are doing in the present deeds,
That all your acts are queens.

One sees why Florizel might take the risk of "a wild dedication of yourselves / To unpath'd waters, undream'd shores." Rosalie Colie usefully traced some of the Shakespearean originalities in regard to pastoral conventions here. I myself would emphasize how little really any conventions of pastoral suit either Perdita's art-exalted nature or Florizel's as he is influenced by her. Perdita incants more like a mortal goddess, Flora, than like an earthly maiden, while the inspired Florizel celebrates her like an Elizabethan John Keats. It takes an extraordinary effort to keep in mind that Perdita is invoking absent flowers, rather than actual, natural presences. Those "daffadils, violets, primroses, oxlips, lilies" are not seasonal, due to Proserpina's failure of nerve, and so Perdita's great declaration is a kind of litany of negations, and yet makes a wholly positive effect, upon the audience as upon her lover. When she cries out, with marvelous boldness: "Come, take your flow'rs," she substitutes her own body for the floral tribute she has conveyed only through its absence. Startled as she herself is by her unaccustomed and only apparent lack of modesty, she provokes Florizel's ecstatic defense of her ontological goodness, as it were. I can think of no comparable praise by a lover to his beloved, anywhere in Western literature since the song that was Solomon's.

The deepest aesthetic puzzle (and strength) of *The Winter's Tale* remains its extraordinary originality, striking even for Shakespeare. In a drama where everything is incongruous, everything works together to conclude in a new mode of congruity:

If this be magic, let it be an art
Lawful as eating.

If eating has become yet another art that itself is Nature, then we tremble on the verge of an aesthetic that, by magic, will consume Nature. Jealousy will vanish away, and with it our darkest tendency, which is to react to any declaration that we are alive, by hooting at it, like an old tale. *The Winter's Tale* evidently exists to tell us that, it appears, we live, though yet we speak not.

"Great Creating Nature": An Essay on *The Winter's Tale*

G. Wilson Knight

> But some man will say, How are the dead raised up? and with what
> body do they come? Thou fool, that which thou sowest is not quickened,
> except it die; and that which thou sowest, thou sowest not that body that
> shall be, but bare grain, it may chance of wheat, or of some other grain: but
> God giveth it a body as it hath pleased him, and to every seed his own
> body.
>
>   All flesh is not the same flesh; but there is one kind of flesh of men,
> another flesh of beasts, another of fishes and another of birds. There are
> also celestial bodies and bodies terrestrial: but the glory of the celestial is one,
> and the glory of the terrestrial is another. There is one glory of the sun,
> and another glory of the moon, and another glory of the stars; for one star
> differeth from another star in glory. So also is the resurrection of the dead.
>
> I Corinthians 15:35

In *The Winter's Tale* Shakespeare handles a similar narrative to that of *Pericles* with the infusion of a closer and more realistic human concern and a tightening of dramatic conflict. Pericles experiences a sense of evil followed by unmerited suffering; Leontes sins and endures a purgatory of guilt. Here the sackcloth and ashes of Pericles' martyrdom are given a profounder relevance.

The Winter's Tale has had a poor showing in commentary, having seldom been regarded as more than an inconsequential romance with fine bits of poetry; while even those who, during recent years, have regarded it as a serious reading of human affairs, have avoided, or slurred over, as though un-at-home with its nature, the

---

From *The Crown of Life: Essays in Interpretation of Shakespeare's Final Plays.* © 1958 by Methuen & Co. Ltd.

crucial and revealing event to which the whole action moves: the resurrection of Hermione.

The play is in three main sections. The first is tragic; the second pastoral; the third must for the present be left undefined. There is a strong suggestion throughout of season-myth, with a balance of summer against winter. Evil passions, storm, and ship-wreck are contrasted with young love and humour. Maturity and death are set against birth and resurrection.

The action opens with a short prose dialogue between Camillo and Archidamus in which the simplicities of Bohemia are contrasted with the luxuries of Sicilia. The contrast is not later developed, and more important are the following remarks on maturity and youth. Leontes and Polixenes "were trained together in their childhoods," though since separated by "mature" responsibilities (1.1.24–35). The picture is completed by thought of the boy Mamillius:

> CAMILLO: It is a gallant child; one that indeed physics the subject, makes old hearts fresh; they that went on crutches ere he was born desire yet their life to see him a man.
> ARCHIDAMUS: Would they else be content to die?
>
> (1.1.42)

Youth is conceived as a power; as a renewer of life and antagonist to death. Thus early is the central theme of *The Winter's Tale* set before us.

Polixenes also has a son whom he "longs to see" (1.1.34), but Hermione presses his stay, asking about his and her own lord's youth together and of their "tricks" as "pretty lordings." He answers:

> POLIXENES: We were, fair queen,
>   Two lads that thought there was no more
>   behind
>   But such a day to-morrow as to-day,
>   And to be boy eternal.
> HERMIONE: Was not my lord the verier wag o' the two?
> POLIXENES: We were as twinn'd lambs that did frisk i'
>   the sun,
>   And bleat the one at the other; what we
>   chang'd
>   Was innocence for innocence; we knew not

> The doctrine of ill-doing, no nor dream'd
> That any did. Had we pursued that life,
> And our weak spirits ne'er been higher rear'd
> With stronger blood, we should have answer'd
>   heaven
> Boldly, "not guilty"; the imposition clear'd
> Hereditary ours.
>
> (1.2.62)

The "eternal" consciousness of childhood is distinguished from the sin-born time-consciousness of man. Polixenes' second speech defines a golden-age existence free from that "hereditary" taint of fallen humanity which appears with the "stronger blood," or passions, of maturity. Leontes, called from his reverie, excuses himself in similar terms; for he has been half-meditating and half-talking to Mamillius, calling him a "calf" and saying how he needs "a rough pash and the shoots that I have" to be like his father (1.2.128–29):

> LEONTES: Looking on the lines
> Of my boy's face, methoughts I did recoil
> Twenty-three years, and saw myself
>   unbreech'd,
> In my green velvet coat, my dagger muzzled,
> Lest it should bite its master, and so prove,
> As ornaments oft do, too dangerous:
> How like, methought, I then was to this
>   kernel,
> This squash, this gentleman. Mine honest
>   friend,
> Will you take eggs for money?
> MAMILLIUS: No, my lord, I'll fight.
>
> (1.2.154)

"Calf," "kernel," "squash," "eggs" (also "eggs" earlier at 1.2.131): impressions of young life—remember the frisking lambs of Polixenes' speech—on the various natural planes cluster. Polixenes, questioned as to his own "young prince" (1.2.164), answers:

> POLIXENES: If at home, sir,
> He's all my exercise, my mirth, my matter,

> Now my sworn friend and then mine enemy;
> My parasite, my soldier, statesman, all:
> He makes a July day short as December,
> And with his varying childness cures in me
> Thoughts that would thick my blood.

LEONTES: So stands this squire
Offic'd with me.

(1.2.165)

All humanity is compacted in the loved person, after the manner of Helena's "Not my virginity yet . . ." in *All's Well That Ends Well* (1.1.181). Childhood is shown as a redeeming force, subduing horrors. Mamillius is, at the play's start, dramatically central. Defined mainly by what is said to, or about, him, and especially by Leontes' by-play ("What, hast smutch'd thy nose?" at 1.2.122), "my young rover" (1.2.176) focalizes the poetry of boyhood and fills the stage.

This poetry is, however, countered by Leontes' rising jealousy conceived as evil in contrast to the golden-age of childhood. Leontes lives in the world of mature passion with attendant knowledge of evil, and consequent suspicion. More, his suspicion is an ugly thing, itself an evil; it is, practically, sin. The central emphasis in Shakespeare on conjugal trust and fidelity is patent: the deepest issues of good and evil are through it expressed. From Provençal lyric, through Petrarch, to Dante, romantic love is haloed with semi-divine meaning. At the Renaissance there is a further development: the romantic idea descends from fancy to actuality; it becomes practical, and therefore moral, in the ethic of marriage. Now the dramatic implications of this change have received insufficient notice. Spenser's doctrine of marriage-love is less important than Lyly's dramatization of it: in Lyly the happy-ending love-drama, or love-ritual, not only releases drama from ecclesiastical domination but sets it firmly on a new course, which it follows still, thereby witnessing the unexhausted meaning, social and religious, of this persistent theme. In Shakespeare love-integrity is all but the supreme good, in both comedy and tragedy, the pattern being especially clear in *Othello*, with Desdemona as divinity and Iago as devil. Now, whatever our private social tenets, we must, in reading *The Winter's Tale*, be prepared to accept the Shakespearian emphasis as a preliminary to understanding. Great poetry seldom leaps direct at universal ideas for their own sake; its ideas are housed in flesh and blood; and there is a logic of incarnated thought, a blood-contact and descent from body to body, that does not necessarily correspond point by point to any conceptual chain. So, though Shakespeare writes here as a poet of the Renaissance as it specifically shaped itself in England, with a plot-interest confined to suspicion of conjugal infidelity, the radiations set going concern the very essence of evil; sexual jealousy is shown as a concentration of possessiveness and inferiority developing into malice with Leontes' suspicion aptly enough called "sin" (1.2.283) and the whole argument considered a matter of "good and evil" (1.2.303). But opposite the hero stands his own child, whose very being is a wisdom and an assurance:

> MAMILLIUS: I am like you, they say.
> LEONTES: Why, that's some comfort.
>
> (1.2.207)

The boy has broken into one of his father's interjectory paroxysms. The remark and Leontes' reaction are simple enough; but the dramatic context is already so loaded with meaning that the simplicity reverberates beyond itself. *The Winter's Tale* is more than a "morality" play; and yet, with no loss of sharp human particularization, Mamillius stands before Leontes as Truth confronting Error.

Leontes is shown as a man inwardly tormented. His misery expresses itself in short, stabbing sentences of great force:

> Too hot, too hot!
> To mingle friendship far is mingling bloods.
> I have *tremor cordis* on me: my heart dances:
> But not for joy; not joy.
>
> (1.2.109)

His words jet from a similar nervous disorganization to that less vividly expressed in Macbeth's

> Why do I yield to that suggestion
> Whose horrid image does unfix my hair,
> And makes my seated heart knock at my ribs
> Against the use of nature?
>
> (*Macbeth* 1.3.134)

Leontes' early soliloquies contrast with his, and others', conversation when a more reasonable intercourse is demanded; he can mask his feelings. But, left to himself, his anguish comes out in hisses, jets of poison, carried over by sibilants and thoughts of stagnant water:

> Gone already!
> Inch-thick, knee-deep, o'er head and ears a fork'd one!
> Go play, boy, play; thy mother plays, and I
> Play too, but so disgrac'd a part, whose issue
> Will hiss me to my grave: contempt and clamour
> Will be my knell. Go play, boy, play. There have been
> Or I am much deceiv'd, cuckolds ere now;
> And many a man there is even at this present,
> Now, while I speak this, holds his wife by the arm,
> That little thinks she has been sluic'd in's absence,
> And his pond fish'd by his next neighbour, by
> Sir Smile, his neighbour

> (1.2.185)

The word "hiss" occurs as a threat, drawing close. Hermione is "slippery" (1.2.273). How poignantly the slime of this reptilian horror coiling round Leontes is countered by the little boy's presence, leading to the ugly dexterity of the wit on "play."

The spasmodic jerks of his language reflect Leontes' unease: he is, as it were, being sick; ejecting a poison, which yet grows stronger; something he has failed to digest, assimilate. Images of nausea pour out. His marriage is "spotted," like a toad (cp. "most toad-spotted traitor" at *King Lear* 5.3.140; and Othello's "I had rather be a toad" and "cistern for foul toads to knot and gender in" at *Othello* 3.3.270 and 4.2.60); and this defilement is to him "goads, thorns, nettles, tails of wasps" (1.2.328–29). Our most virulent speech of disgust involves the much-loathed spider:

> There may be in the cup
> A spider steep'd, and one may drink, depart,
> And yet partake no venom, for his knowledge
> Is not infected; but if one present
> The abhorr'd ingredient to his eye, make known
> How he hath drunk, he cracks his gorge, his sides,
> With violent hefts. I have drunk, and seen the spider.

> (2.1.38)

The studied build-up of the preceding lines injects a maximum of force into that final, icy reserve. Indeed, Leontes' most vitriolic spasms get themselves out with a certain under-emphasis, not unlike Swift's general expression of nausea through *meiosis*; as though the extreme of satiric bitterness were always loath to risk suicide in the *katharsis* of luxuriant expression. Leontes' paroxysms never enjoy Othello's even swell and surge of fully developed emotion:

> Come, sir page,
> Look on me with your welkin eye: sweet villain!
> Most dear'st! my collop! Can thy dam?—may't be?—
> Affection! thy intention stabs the centre:
> Thou dost make possible things not so held,
> Communicat'st with dreams;—how can this be?—
> With what's unreal thou coactive art,
> And fellow'st nothing: then, 'tis very credent
> Thou may'st co-join with something; and thou dost,
> And that beyond commission, and I find it,
> And that to the infection of my brains
> And hardening of my brows.
>
> (1.2.136)

From the boy and his "welkin eye"—a phrase enlisting all great nature's serenity and light—Leontes is being swiftly projected into instability; the universal "centre" is gone, stabbed by this supposed "affection" (i.e. growing love) of Hermione and Polixenes. The result is nightmare. The impossible has happened: worse, it is even now happening; the known creation has had dallyings with the "unreal," the "nothing," and thence given birth (as in *Macbeth*) to an only-too-real action of hideous obscenity in the visible order. We are close to Macbeth's "horrible imaginings" of his own as yet "fantastical" crime, with "function smother'd in surmise" until "nothing is but what is not" (*Macbeth* 1.3.137–42). In both plays we have evil impinging as essential "nothing," unreality, a delirium, which yet most violently acts on the real. Leontes' whirling sequence rises to the powerful and revealing "infection of my brains" —thereby half-admitting his own now poisoned thinking—and then drops into an understress, almost euphemism, in "hardening of my brows." And yet that last reserve again reflects a state the very opposite of repose: that of a man tense, nerving himself to believe, to endure—more, to *be*—the hideous, horned, thing. We are nearer *Macbeth* than *Othello*.

This spasmodic, interjectory, explosive style, however, whirls itself once into a single rhythmic movement of towering excellence, developing the "nothing" of our last quotation into a truly shattering reality. "Is whispering nothing?" asks Leontes of Camillo, and continues with a list of love's advances, jerked out in rapid fire, and concluding:

> Is this nothing?
> Why, then the world and all that's in't is nothing;
> The covering sky is nothing; Bohemia nothing;
> My wife is nothing; nor nothing have these nothings,
> If this be nothing.
>
> (1.2.292)

Nature's "centre" and "welkin" (sky) in the boy's eye (cp. "the eye of Heaven" for the sun in Sonnet 18) were first (in our former speech) contrasted with "nothing"; here the nihilistic horror itself assumes validity equal to that of the "world" and "covering sky": this contrast or identity (as Leontes claims) is, as we shall see, basic. Great nature is here our final term of reference, to which even evil must appeal, somewhat as Hamlet, from the depths of his melancholia, admits the firmamental splendour.

The victory of evil in Leontes' soul, its rise in philosophical status, is thus here matched, though only for an instant, by a corresponding mastery of rhythm, rather as in Macbeth's later speeches. One must beware of regarding tormented rhythms as a poetical goal. Possibly we over-rate Shakespeare's rough-handling of language to correspond to the twists and jerks of psychic experience, not unlike the helter-skelter impressionism brought to a self-conscious art by the justly praised and influential Hopkins. One can often approve a poet's disrespect to the tyrannies of rhythm and syntax; but there are dangers. Though Shakespeare indeed uses such a crammed, often cramped, manner elsewhere, the style is certainly most effective when expressing nightmare or disintegration: disrupted rhythms suit Brutus's and Macbeth's soliloquies before their half-intended murders (*Julius Caesar* 2.1.10–34; *Macbeth* 1.7.1–12). Shakespeare later allows himself more and more freedom in a manner which is perilously near to mannerism; and where no especial disorder, psychic or—as in a messenger-speech (as at

Cymbeline 5.3.14–51)—physical is concerned, the result can irritate. With Leontes, however, the purpose has been patent; the disrupted style not merely fits, it explores and exposes the anguish depicted.

That anguish is hell. Leontes half knows, too, that it is sin. He goes to Camillo, if not for absolution, at least for confirmation and collaboration:

> I have trusted thee, Camillo,
> With all the nearest things to my heart, as well
> My chamber-councils, wherein, priest-like, thou
> Hast cleans'd my bosom: I from thee departed
> Thy penitent reform'd. But we have been
> Deceiv'd in thy integrity, deceiv'd
> In that which seems so.
>
> (1.2.235)

He wants Camillo to corroborate his own discovery. He is nervous, tentative; something intimate is, as the confessional phraseology hints, involved. But he is not asking advice; the least hint of disagreement rouses his fury. Indeed, he now positively wants his suspicions, which have become the dearest part of him, confirmed:

> CAMILLO: Good my lord, be cur'd
> Of this diseas'd opinion, and betimes;
> For 'tis most dangerous.
> LEONTES: Say it be, 'tis true.
> CAMILLO: No, no, my lord.
> LEONTES: It is; you lie, you lie;
> I say thou liest, Camillo, and I hate thee;
> Pronounce thee a gross lout, a mindless slave
>
> (1.2.296)

The phrase "diseas'd opinion" is exact: Leontes seems to admit disease, whilst insisting on his suspicion's truth. Opposition raises a devil of self-defensive fury, rising to bombast and that type of vulgar abuse so often symptomatic of a semi-conscious guilt.

His evil is self-born and unmotivated. Commentators have searched in vain for "motives" to explain the soul-states and actions of Hamlet, Iago and Macbeth, without realizing that the poet is concerned not with trivialities, but with evil itself, whose cause remains as dark as theology: given a "sufficient" motive, the thing to be studied vanishes. In Leontes we have a study of evil yet more

coherent, realistic and compact; a study of almost demonic possession. He reacts violently to criticism: when Antigonus and others
presume to argue, he shouts "Hold your peaces!" (2.1.138); and
when he hears that Paulina is outside, Paulina who is to function
throughout as his accuser, almost as his conscience, he starts "like a
guilty thing upon a fearful summons" (*Hamlet* 1.1.148), as though
recognizing his natural enemy:

> How!
> Away with that audacious lady! Antigonus,
> I charg'd thee that she should not come about me.
> I knew she would.
>
> (2.3.41)

The last words have the very accent of neurosis, blackening with
defensive scorn the good onto which it projects its own evil.

Leontes dimly recognizes that he is behaving as a tyrant,
using position and power to bolster up and enforce on others a
disease in himself. He is accordingly at pains to show himself
as relying on his lords' advice on condition that they do not
oppose him:

> Why, what need we
> Commune with you of this, but rather follow
> Our forceful instigation? Our prerogative
> Calls not your counsels, but our natural goodness
> Imparts this.
>
> (2.1.160)

He is insecure enough to want support, would convince himself of
"natural goodness"; but, failing support, will go his own way.
However, he has sent to the Oracle of Apollo for "greater confirmation," realizing the danger of rashness and wishing to "give rest
to the minds of others" (2.1.179–92). Tyrant though he be, he can
still think constitutionally. Though absolutely certain, he is yet not
quite certain that his certainty can maintain itself: paradoxes abound.
He is on a rack of indecision:

> Nor night, nor day, no rest; it is but weakness
> To bear the matter thus; mere weakness. If
> The cause were not in being,—part o' the cause,
> She the adultress; for the harlot king
> Is quite beyond mine arm, plot-proof; but she

> I can hook to me: say, that she were gone,
> Given to the fire, a moiety of my rest
> Might come to me again.
>
> (2.3.1)

In the full flood of anger, when his lords kneel, imploring him to spare the new-born child, he is indecisive and gives ground, muttering: "I am a feather for each wind that blows" (2.3.153). We cannot admire him, as we admire Richard III, the later Macbeth, and Milton's Satan, for a whole-hearted Satanism. Nor can we sympathize, as with Othello. The emotion aroused is rather a stern pity. He himself knows that to be mistaken in such a matter were "piteous" (2.1.181; cp. also 3.2.235). More, it is almost comic: Antigonus suggests that the public scandal will raise everyone "to laughter" (2.1.197). Indeed, of all Shakespeare's jealous husbands Leontes is nearest to Ford, existing in almost comic objectivity, though without one atom's loss of tragic intensity. We have in him a sharp personification of the blend so obvious in the wider design.

Tyranny and superstition are mutually related. Tyranny is the forceful domination of a person in the semi-evil, semi-neurotic, state of contemporary humanity. Were the tyrant purely integrated, his absolute control might be a good; hence the will in all royalist states to see the king as a superman of goodness and wisdom, and the theological equation of Christ = King. The tyrant, however, makes power serve personal error, opening the way for a number of illegitimate powers; at the extreme, superstitious belief regarding the manipulation of natural forces, and finally for beings of an infra-natural kind. In Shakespeare's two full-length studies of tyranny in *Richard III* and *Macbeth* the emphasis on ill-omened creatures, witchcraft, and ghosts is thoroughly integral.

Now Leontes has, without knowing it, entered this domain; and, by a transition well known to psychologists, tends to deny vehemently the name of tyrant, whilst seeing in his opposite, Paulina, the exact evil really lodged in himself. She brings from the prison, where his wife lies, Leontes' new-born child-daughter, challenging him with utter fearlessness, reiterating the (to him—since he half fears its truth) maddening phrase "good queen" (2.3.58) and finally stinging him to madness by actual presentation of the child. The opposition of childhood and evil, already made vivid by Mamillius, here reaches its maximum dramatic intensity and rouses in Leontes a devil that speaks directly in terms of black magic. Leontes now sees Paulina as a witch and as she presents the baby shouts: "Out! A mankind witch!" (2.3.67). He is, as Paulina coolly observes, "mad" (2.3.71). His storming gets more violent and excessively ugly:

> Traitors!
> Will you not push her out? Give her the bastard.
> Thou dotard! thou art woman-tired, unroosted
> By thy dame Partlet here. Take up the bastard;
> Take't up, I say; give't to thy crone.
>
> (2.3.72)

Notice the unchivalrous, ugly scorn, the horror almost of woman as woman, in "Partlet" and "crone," the latter suggesting witchcraft; and also the continuation of our political emphasis in "traitors," to be repeated again by "a *nest* of traitors" (2.3.81), subtly suggesting, as does "Partlet" too, a growing identity, in Leontes' diseased mind, of creative nature with treachery. Against his words is Paulina's more religious threat to Antigonus that his hands will be for ever "unvenerable" (2.3.77) if he obeys; and her insistence that "the root" of Leontes' "opinion" is "as rotten as ever oak or stone was sound" (2.3.89), driving home once more the all-important contrast of Leontes' crime with the stabilities of nature. After her exquisite description of nature's handiwork in the child's likeness to its father, Leontes' reply is: "A gross hag!" (2.3.107). The more perfect the good presented, the more black it rises before him; like Milton's Satan, only without knowing it (as Macbeth knows it at the end and by so doing all but redeems himself), Leontes has said, "Evil, be thou my good." His values are all transposed and Paulina deserves a witch's death:

LEONTES: I'll ha' thee burn'd.
PAULINA: I care not;
       It is a heretic that makes the fire,
       Not she which burns in't. I'll not call you
           tyrant;
       But this most cruel usage of your queen—
       Not able to produce more accusation
       Than your own weak-hing'd fancy—something
           savours
       Of tyranny, and will ignoble make you,
       Yea, scandalous to the world.

LEONTES: On your allegiance,
          Out of the chamber with her! Were I a tyrant,
          Where were her life? she durst not call me so
          If she did know me one. Away with her!
                                              (2.3.113)

Paulina's phraseology ("heretic") is again orthodox and Christian. Leontes' "on your allegiance" echoes Lear's scene with Kent (*King Lear* 1.1.122–82), where the psychology of tyranny was, though less subtly developed, very similar. Notice Paulina's reiterated emphasis on tyranny, and Leontes' violent reaction. He fears the thought, half-recognizes its truth; though, with some justice, defending himself *to himself*, adducing rational evidence; trying to crush the summoning conscience whose outward projection is, throughout the play, Paulina. He has, however, sunk deep into paganism, witnessed by his intention to have the child "consum'd with fire" (2.3.133). His emphatic desire to *burn* suggests a complex of tyranny and paganism, not to be finally distinguished from that semi-pagan fear of paganism which led to the tyrannic burning of supposed heretics and witches. There is in both a submission to fear and a desire to leave no trace of the dreaded thing: hence Leontes' earlier thought that if Hermione were "given to the fire" his peace of mind might return (2.3.8); and his recent threat to Paulina. Paulina, in opposition, represents the pure Christian conscience, together with common sense. Aligned with her are (1) the new-born baby and (2) all those natural and human sanctities it symbolizes.

Nature rules our play. Despite the court setting, nature-suggestion has been, from the start, vivid, introduced by Polixenes' opening lines:

          Nine changes of the watery star have been
          The shepherd's note since we have left our throne.
                                              (1.2.1)

The following dialogue is sprinkled with natural imagery in close association with youth—in the description of the two kings as "twinn'd lambs that did frisk i' the sun" (1.2.67), the "unfledg'd days" of boyhood (1.2.78), Leontes' use of steer, heifer, kernel and squash. A general pastoralism rings in the "mort o' the deer" at 1.2.119. Leontes sees his wife's supposed love-making as a bird's holding up of her "bill" (1.2.183); and there are his more obvious animal-images of nausea already noted. Seasons, to be so important in the general design, are suggested by "sneaping winds" at 1.2.13 and twice actually mentioned: Polixenes' son "makes a July's day short as December" (1.2.169), and we have Mamillius's contribution to the play's wintry opening in his unfinished story. "A sad tale," he says, is "best for winter" and continues:

> MAMILLIUS: There was a man—
> HERMIONE: Nay, come, sit down; then on.
> MAMILLIUS: Dwelt by a churchyard. I will tell it softly;
>   Yond crickets shall not hear it.
>
>   (2.1.24–30)

The "sad tale" reflects the oncoming disaster; the boy's words characterize his father, dwelling close (as is hinted by a revealing image at 2.1.150) to death; the broken story is itself a little tragedy. But here all tragedies are firmly held within Nature's vastness. Hermione's thought of how Polixenes may "unsphere the stars with oaths" (1.2.48) repeats the manner of *Antony and Cleopatra*: compare, too, Camillo's "among the infinite doings of the world" (1.2.253) with the Soothsayer's "in nature's infinite book of secrecy a little I can read" at *Antony and Cleopatra*, 1.2.11. Nature here, however, whilst remaining vast, is normally less philosophically, more concretely, present. Three times already (1.2.137–39; 1.2.293–94; 2.3.90) we have found creation's firmamental and earthly steadfastness contrasted with the hideous instabilities of evil; and throughout Leontes' fall that solid "world" and its "covering sky" (1.2.293–94; cp. also his "You'll be found, be you beneath the sky" at 1.2.179) are our touchstones of reality.

The close association of nature and human childhood has Christian affinities, and Christian tonings occur naturally among our positives. We have seen that Paulina employs them. When Polixenes calls Hermione "my most sacred lady" (1.2.76), whilst admitting his own lapse, since childhoood, into "temptations," the adjective goes (as later at 2.3.84 and 5.1.172) beyond formal courtesy. More direct is:

>   O, then my best blood turn
>   To an infected jelly, and my name
>   Be yok'd with his that did betray the Best!
>
>   (1.2.417)

—though the immediate comparison (as at *Richard II* 4.1.170, 240; and *Timon of Athens* 1.2.48–51) still serves a human purpose. But here is something quite new and characteristic, indeed, the most characteristic possible, of *The Winter's Tale*. When the Gaoler doubts whether he should release the new-born baby from the prison without a warrant, Paulina answers:

> You need not fear it, sir:
> The child was prisoner to the womb, and is
> By law and process of great nature thence
> Freed and enfranchis'd.
>
> (2.2.58)

"Freed": how the word contrasts with the stifling atmosphere of Leontes' own enslavement to evil and imprisoning of Hermione. It is precisely this freedom of "great nature," unpossessive, ever-new, creative, against which Leontes' tyranny has offended; and his offence is therefore also one against the natural order whose very laws are those of creation and freedom; and therefore, too, of miracle.

"Great nature" is our over-ruling deity—hence the broad phraseology of "your mother rounds apace" (2.1.16)—responsible for the miraculous perpetuation and re-creation of worn and sinful man. Mamillius's likeness to Leontes is, as we have seen, emphatic; as when, looking on his son, the father remembers his own boyhood (1.2.154–61), or sees the boy's smutched nose as "a copy out of mine" (1.2.123); while Mamillius himself remarks: "I am like you, they say" (1.2.208). The emphasis reaches a climax in Paulina's presentation to the horrified Leontes of his new-born baby. We have had something similar in Mamillius's play with the ladies and his talk of eyebrows (2.1.7–15), but here is a greater passage:

> Behold, my lords,
> Although the print be little, the whole matter
> And copy of the father; eye, nose, lip,
> The trick of's frown, his forehead, nay, the valley,
> The pretty dimples of his chin and cheek, his smiles,
> The very mould and frame of hand, nail, finger:
> And thou, good goddess Nature, which hast made it
> So like to him that got it, if thou hast
> The ordering of the mind too, 'mongst all colours
> No yellow in't; lest she suspect, as he does,
> Her children not her husband's.
>
> (2.3.97)

Notice the pretty irony of "the trick of his frown"; Leontes' ugly wrath at this instant is reflected in the baby's puckered brow. Notice, too, the slight but important reservation as to whether Nature also orders the mind, less an assertion of difference than symptom of the will to drive natural supremacy to the limit, in spite of traditional distinctions which are nevertheless remembered. Observe the exact and objective description of human lineaments, with a maximum of love's intimacy, yet so purified of any clouding, or glamorous, passion or sentimentality that we are nearer to Blake's "minute particulars" than to the physical descriptions in *Venus and Adonis*; and yet the physical is even more intensely, though quietly, preserved; the speech is, of course, maternal rather than erotic. The identification, through love, is so complete that objectivity supervenes with a purity and realism the precise antithesis to the other objectivity of Leontes' hideous command to carry hence "this female bastard" (2.3.174), where the one adjective "female" houses a whole philosophy of cynical materialism. Paulina's speech lives the play's doctrine on the sanctity of human creation and the miraculous doings of "nature": it is thus deeply Christian. Such is the antagonist to Leontes' sin and the tragedy it draws swiftly down; a thing already of such power that Hermione's final resurrection shall be no madness. It is easy to see why Leontes' possessing devil is so violently roused: it recognises its antagonist in the baby. The dark powers in *Macbeth* are similarly opposed by a crowned and tree-bearing child. So our dramatic conflict of delirious evil against the stabilities of nature works through conversations about boyhood and the stage-presence of the attractive Mamillius, to this final opposition, with Paulina as directing agent. Mamillius's presence was always the more eloquent for his few speeches; and the apparently helpless new-born baby (in Wordsworthian phrase "deaf and silent," yet reading "the eternal deep" and "haunted for ever by the eternal mind," in the Immortality Ode) is necessarily even more potent.

Though often Christian in impact, the natural majesty explored is also in part Hellenic, relating directly to our controlling god "great Apollo" (2.3.199), the sun-god, and his oracle at Delphos. Leontes sends "to sacred Delphos, to Apollo's temple" to solicit, in Christian phrase, the god's "spiritual counsel" (2.1.182, 185). Cleomenes and Dion return awestruck, deeply impressed by the island's (it is so considered) "delicate" climate, the "sweet" air and general *fertility* (3.1.1–3; cp. *The Tempest* 2.1.43–49, 55); and even more by the temple, the "celestial habits" and "reverence" of the "grave" priests and the "sacrifice" so "ceremonious, solemn and unearthly"; while the actual voice or "burst" of the oracle was as a terrifying judgement, "kin to Jove's thunder" (3.1.3–11: cp. the thunderous appearances of Jupiter in *Cymbeline*, 5.4.93, and of Ariel in *The Tempest* 3.3.53). They pray that "great Apollo" and the package sealed by "Apollo's great divine" may quickly turn all "to the best" and disclose something "rare" (3.1.14–21); the word "rare," used already at 3.1.13, being frequent on such occasions throughout this and other of the Final Plays (as in "rarest sounds" at *Pericles* 5.1.233). Apollo is both a nature-deity and transcendent; though a god of sun-fire (as is clear later), his revelatory voice makes the hearer "nothing" (3.1.11), the word already used to define Leontes' ghastly experience. Apollo is as mysterious and as awful as Wordsworth's gigantic mountain-presences; he is both the Greek Apollo and the Hebraic Jehovah. In him the play's poetry is personified.

Hermione is brought to trial. Leontes opens the proceedings with a disclaimer:

> Let us be clear'd
> Of being tyrannous, since we so openly
> Proceed in justice.
>
> (3.2.4)

His fear, as before, marks a recognition; the tyranny in his soul he would film over by a show of judicial procedure. Hermione's defence is characterized by lucidity and reason; her "integrity" (3.2.27) is in every syllable; she is expostulating as with a nervous invalid. She wields a martyr-like strength:

> But thus: if powers divine
> Behold our human actions, as they do,
> I doubt not then but innocence shall make
> False accusation blush, and tyranny
> Tremble at patience.
>
> (3.2.29)

She aims to increase his already obvious discomfort; that is, to appeal to his "conscience" (3.2.47). She is being condemned by his "dreams" (3.2.82); we should say "fantasies." Her language grows more and more coldly convincing:

> Sir, spare your threats:
> The bug which you would fright me with I seek.
> To me can life be no commodity:
> The crown and comfort of my life, your favour,
> I do give lost; for I do feel it gone,
> But know not how it went. My second joy,
> And first-fruits of my body, from his presence
> I am barr'd, like one infectious. My third comfort,
> Starr'd most unluckily, is from my breast,
> The innocent milk in its most innocent mouth,
> Hail'd out to murder.
>
> (3.2.92)

Notice the vivid physical perception and nature-feeling in "first-fruits" and "milk"; we shall find such phrases elsewhere. The calm yet condemnatory scorn of Hermione's manner shows a close equivalence to that of Queen Katharine on trial in *Henry VIII* (2.4). Both are daughters of a foreign king suffering in a strange home. Hermione is "a great king's daughter" (3.2.40), daughter of "the emperor of Russia" (3.2.120–24): compare *Henry VIII* 2.4.13, 46; 3.1.81–82, 142–50. Both appeal, with a similarly climactic effect, to the highest known authority, Queen Katharine to the Pope and Hermione to the Oracle:

> but for mine honour
> Which I would free, if I shall be condemn'd
> Upon surmises, all proofs sleeping else
> But what your jealousies awake, I tell you
> 'Tis rigour and not law. Your honours all,
> I do refer me to the oracle:
> Apollo be my judge!
>
> (3.2.111)

The request is granted by one of the lords: in the ritual of both trials the King is half felt as a subject before the majesty of law.

So Cleomenes and Dion swear on a "sword of justice" (3.2.125) that the "holy seal" (3.2.130) is intact; and the package is opened. Hermione and Polixenes are cleared and Leontes revealed as "a jealous tyrant," who must live "without an heir if that which is lost be not found" (3.2.133–37). Truth is thus vindicated by the voice of supreme judgement accusing Leontes of lawless tyranny; but the devil in him is not easily exorcised. At first he will not submit; asserts blasphemously that "there is no truth at all in the oracle" (3.2.141); probably seizes the paper and tears it to shreds, insisting that the trial continue, thereby revealing his utter subjection of justice to the egotistic will. But now, following sharply on his impious disregard, comes news of Mamillius's death. No dramatic incident in Shakespeare falls with so shattering an impact; no reversal is more poignant than when, after a moment's dazedness, Leontes' whole soul-direction changes:

> Apollo's angry; and the heavens themselves
> Do strike at my injustice.
>
> (3.2.147)

Great nature, the giver of children, can as easily recall them: that nature is, here, the transcendent Apollo, who both guides and judges. Leontes' crime, be it noted, is one of "injustice." Hermione faints and is taken away by Paulina.

Leontes next speaks two revealing phrases: "I have," he mutters, "too much believed mine own suspicion"; he admits "being transported by my jealousies" (3.2.152, 159). He has allowed himself to be temporarily possessed, dominated, by something in himself which, given power, has "transported" him, that is, changed his nature as by magic (cp. "translated" at *A Midsummer Night's Dream* 3.1.125). By this inward usurpation the essence of tyranny and injustice has lodged in him, only to be exorcised by the violent impact of his crime's actual result: Mamillius's illness was first brought on by Hermione's disgrace (2.3.13–17). Now Leontes, having awakened from his delirious dream, speaks with a new simplicity:

> Apollo, pardon
> My great profaneness 'gainst thine oracle!
> I'll reconcile me to Polixenes,
> New woo my queen, recall the good Camillo.
>
> (3.2.154)

But his punishment is not over. Paulina returns, and with a long speech of considered vehemence says exactly what wants saying, because now only can its import register:

What studied torments, tyrant, hast for me?
What wheels? racks? fires? What flaying? or what
        boiling
In leads, or oils? what old or newer torture
Must I receive, whose every word deserves
To taste of thy most worst?

(3.2.176)

Suggestion of tyranny here reaches its climax; though Paulina refers to "thy tyranny together working with thy jealousies" (3.2.180), they are two aspects of one reality, one complex, from which Leontes' actions have flowed. Paulina, comparing him to a devil (3.2.193), lists his crimes, with bitter irony suggesting (what is a half-truth) that they are none of them his fault; and concluding with news of Hermione's death and a demand for vengeance from Heaven. Throughout, she is playing on his conscience; more—she is his conscience.

Hermione, she says, is dead, and the man who could resurrect her must needs be worshipped as a god (3.2.208):

But, O thou tyrant!
Do not repent these things, for they are heavier
Than all thy woes can stir; therefore betake thee
To nothing but despair. A thousand knees
Ten thousand years together, naked, fasting
Upon a barren mountain, and still winter
In storm perpetual, could not move the gods
To look that way thou wert.

(3.2.208)

The association of winter and penitence, though not itself new (see *Love's Labour's Lost* 5.2.798–815), assumes here a new precision. Paulina's voice, so hated before, now matches Leontes' own thoughts and is accordingly desired:

Go on, go on;
Thou can'st not speak too much: I have deserv'd
All tongues to talk their bitterest.

(3.2.215)

Rebuked for her forwardness, she answers:

> I am sorry for't:
> All faults I make, when I shall come to know them
> I do repent.
>
> (3.2.219)

She is, indeed, repentance incarnate: that is her dramatic office. Now she recognizes that Leontes is "touch'd to the noble heart" (3.2.222), nobility, in the chivalric tradition, involving Christian virtues; but, in apologizing for reminding him of what he "should forget," she only further defines her office; and the more she emphasizes and lists the sorrows she will not refer to, the loss of Leontes' queen and children, as well as her own lord, the more she drives home on him his grief (3.2.223–33). He, however, prefers "truth" to "pity"; would live into, perhaps through, the purgation of remorse; and ends speaking of the "chapel" where his queen and son are to be buried, and where he will attend in sorrow so long as "nature" gives him strength (3.2.233–43). His last words hold a subdued dignity; his speech is calm and lucid; he is now, as never before, kingly.

No full-length Shakespearian tragedy reaches the intensity of these three acts: they move with a whirling, sickening, speed. Leontes is more complex than Othello as a study of jealousy and more realistically convincing than Macbeth as a study of evil possession. In him are blended the Renaissance, man-born, evil projected through Iago and the medieval supernaturalism of the Weird Sisters. He and his story also include both the personal, family, interest of *Othello* and the communal, tyrannic, theme of *Macbeth*, whilst defining their relation; that is, the relation of emotional and sexual unhealth to tyranny; hence the repeated emphasis here on "tyrant" and the opposing concepts of justice and constitutional law. Macbeth's crime is an act of lustful possessiveness to be contrasted (as I have shown at length in *The Imperial Theme* and *The Shakespearian Tempest*) with the creative kingship of Banquo in association with child-images and nature; while conjugal jealousy is a concentrated exaggeration of domestic ownership and domination, sexually impelled. Clearly each dramatic theme is enriched by mingling with the other, and indeed we find Leontes marking an advance in Shakespeare's human delineation: the poetic and philosophic overtones of Hamlet, Lear and Timon are compressed into a study as sharply defined as the Nurse in *Romeo and Juliet* and as objectively diagnosed as Ford, Malvolio and Parolles. Hence the violent detonation.

The play's morality interest, though less surface-patent than that of *Pericles*, will be clear. But a warning is necessary. Though Shakespeare writes, broadly speaking, from a Christian standpoint, and though christianized phraseology recurs, yet the poet is rather to be supposed as using Christian concepts than as dominated by them. They are implemental to his purpose; but so too are "great Apollo" and "great nature," sometimes themselves approaching Biblical feeling (with Apollo as Jehovah), yet diverging also, especially later, into a pantheism of such majesty that orthodox apologists may well be tempted to call it Christian too; but it is scarcely orthodox. *The Winter's Tale* remains a creation of the Renaissance, that is, of the questing imagination, firmly planted, no doubt, in medieval tradition, but not directed by it. There is a distinction here of importance.

And now, as an echo to our court-tragedy, our action enters, as it were, the elemental background of all tragedy; the wild and rugged Bohemian coast, with threatening storm. We are behind the scenes, where the organizing powers fabricate our human plot. The skies are ominous, as though Heaven were angry at the work in hand (3.3.3–5), for Antigonus, exactly obeying Leontes' command, has brought the child to this "remote and desert place," where "chance may nurse or end it" (2.3.175, 182). It is to be thrown on the mercies of nature:

> Come on, poor babe:
> Some powerful spirit instruct the kites and ravens
> To be thy nurses! Wolves and bears, they say,
> Casting their savageness aside have done
> Like offices of pity.
>
> (2.3.184)

The ruling powers have, however, themselves taken charge, directing Antigonus to this fierce and rugged spot. "Their sacred wills be done" (3.3.7), he says. He recounts how Hermione has appeared to him in a dream, "in pure white robes, like very sanctity"—again a forecast of Queen Katharine—so that he regarded her as a "spirit" come from the "dead"; and tells how she directed him to leave the child in Bohemia. The dream was so convincing that it seemed more real than "slumber"; and he therefore deduces that Hermione "hath suffer'd death" and that, the child being in truth Polixenes', it is Apollo's will it be left in his kingdom (3.3.15–45). He is wrong about the child, but right about Hermione; or again wrong as to both. His ghostly account, with its suggestion of present deity, is the more powerful for the inhuman grandeur of its setting. So, either "for life or death," he leaves the baby upon the "earth" of this inhospitable place; buries it, as a seed, to live or die, praying, "Blossom, speed thee well"; entrusting it to forces beyond man's control, while hoping that the treasure he leaves may help to "breed" it (3.3.40–48). The child is enduring, as it were, a second birth, with the attendant risks, the synchronization of storm and birth recalling *Pericles*. The spot is, as we have been told, famous for its beasts of prey. The storm starts and Antigonus is chased off by a bear.

The incident is as crude as the sudden entry of pirates in *Pericles*. But, as so often there, Shakespeare is moulding events from his own past imagery. His recurrent association of tempests with rough beasts, especially bears (as at *King Lear* 3.4.9–11), is here actualized: the storm starts, the bear appears, and we have a description of shipwreck. We must take the bear seriously, as suggesting man's insecurity in face of untamed nature; indeed, mortality in general.

This scene is a hinge not only for the story but also for the life-views it expresses. We are plunged first into the abysmal smithies below or behind creation, in touch with ghostly presences and superhuman powers; but next, as one dream dissolves into another, we pass from horror to simple, rustic, comedy. We met a precisely similar transition in *Pericles*, where the fishermen fulfilled an office closely resembling that of the Shepherd and Clown here: in both homely rusticity is synchronized and contrasted with storm and shipwreck. There is, however, no satire here in the rustics' talk, except for the Shepherd's opening remark on the behaviour of men between sixteen and three and twenty, always "getting wenches with child, wronging the ancientry, stealing, fighting" (3.3.58–62), which recalls Thersites, whilst continuing our present obsession with birth and age; but there is no more of it. More important are the two lost sheep which he expects to find by the sea "browsing of ivy" (3.3.68): it is somehow very reassuring to find the simple fellow at his homely job after our recent terrors with their appalling sense of human insecurity. Both the Shepherd and his son are thoroughly at home in this weird place; its awe-inspiring quality fades, as memory of nightmare before the heavy step and traffic of dawn. Bears are no terror to them, they know their ways: "they are never curst but when they are hungry" (3.3.135). The scene wakes into semi-humorous prose, sturdy commonsense, and simple kindliness.

There is the usual mismanagement of words typical of Shakespeare's clowns, but the humour soon takes a new turn in the son's exquisite description of the wreck and Antigonus's death, subtly veiling the horror and removing its sting. Tragedy is confronted by comedy working in close alliance with birth:

> Heavy matters! heavy matters! but look thee here, boy.
> Now bless thyself: thou mettest with things dying, I with
> things new born.
>
> (3.3.115)

The baby is found with a casket of gold. The Shepherd calls it a "changeling" and attributes his luck to the "fairies" (3.3.121–22). So the craggy setting is lit by the glow of "fairy gold" (3.3.127). We have entered a new, and safer, world.

Our final summing movement takes us back to Sicilia, where all the people foregather and the complications are resolved.

Leontes is a figure of accomplished repentance. From now on religious phraseology is insistent, with strong Christian tonings:

> Sir, you have done enough, and have perform'd
> A saint-like sorrow; no fault could you make
> Which you have not redeem'd; indeed, paid down
> More penitence than done trespass. At the last,
> Do as the heavens have done, forget your evil;
> With them forgive yourself.
>
> (5.1.1)

His kingdom, as the oracle foretold, is, through his own sin, heirless (5.1.10). The contrast in *Macbeth* between tyranny without issue and Banquo's descendants may assist our response to Leontes' punishment. Both heroes offend against creation and are accordingly themselves uncreative. Paulina stands beside him, a perpetual reminder, referring to Hermione as "she you kill'd" (5.1.15):

LEONTES: I think so. Kill'd!
          She I kill'd! I did so; but thou strik'st me
          Sorely to say I did; it is as bitter
          Upon thy tongue as in my thought. Now,
              good now
          Say so but seldom.

                                        (5.1.16)

Paulina is here to personify Leontes' "thought." Cleomenes, who cannot be expected to consider her dramatic office, rebuffs her sharply; and Dion, in a speech (5.1.24–34) loaded with regal and religious impressions ("sovereign name," "his highness," "royalty," "holy," "holier"), urges the King to marry to beget an heir. Paulina, however, demands respect to the gods' "secret purposes" and the oracle of "divine Apollo," which asserted that Leontes should remain heirless till his child was found (5.1.35–40); and he, wishing he had always followed her counsel, agrees, while further imagining Hermione's return, in accusation. His remarriage, he says,

                    Would make her sainted spirit
          Again possess her corpse and on this stage—
          Where we're offenders now—appear soul-vex'd,
          And begin, "Why to me?"

                                        (5.1.57)

The world of sinful men is widely conceived; but also, ever so delicately, Hermione's return is hinted. Paulina next suggests that had his dead queen "such power" (5.1.60) of return, she would have full "cause" of anger. Where she, Paulina, the ghost, she would shriek, point to his second wife's eyes, calling out, like the ghost in *Hamlet*, "Remember mine" (5.1.67):

LEONTES: Stars, stars!
          And all eyes else dead coals.
                        (5.1.67)

Leontes sits almost tranced, in a state of other-worldly remembrance, all but outside the temporal dimension. Paulina continues to play with the thought of Hermione's return. Leontes is not to marry

> unless another
> As like Hermione as is her picture,
> Affront his eye.
>
> (5.1.73)

His new wife shall be, she says, older than the first:

> She shall be such
> As, walk'd your first queen's ghost, it should take joy
> To see her in your arms.
>
> (5.1.79)

Leontes enters into the grave game, willingly agreeing not to marry till Paulina bids him, and she clinches the compact, whilst further preparing for the resurrection:

> That
> Shall be when your first queen's again in breath;
> Never till then.
>
> (5.1.82)

Observe how carefully we are being prepared for the conclusion, our thoughts whetted, our minds subtly habituated, if not to its possibility, at least to its conceivability.

On the entry of Florizel and Perdita our most important impressions concern Perdita herself, given the usual praise accorded these later heroines: she is "the rarest of all women" (5.1.112), a "goddess" (5.1.131), a "paragon" (5.1.153), or—exactly suiting our recurring impressionism of earth and sun—"the most peerless piece of earth" "that e'er the sun shone bright on" (5.1.94). She reminds the tactless but purposeful Paulina of that "jewel of children," Mamillius (5.1.117). She is a creature

> Would she begin a sect, might quench the zeal
> Of all professors else, make proselytes
> Of who she but bid follow.
>
> (5.1.107)

Earthly and transcendental impressions intermix in her praise. Both recur together in Leontes':

> And you, fair princess—goddess! O, alas!
> I lost a couple, that 'twixt heaven and earth
> Might thus have stood begetting wonder as
> You, gracious couple, do.
>
> (5.1.131)

Children, planted between heaven and earth, beget "wonder," a word to be used later on for miraculous events. Children are copies of their parents:

> Your mother was most true to wedlock, prince;
> For she did print your royal father off,
> Conceiving you.
>
> (5.1.124)

We remember Mamillius's resemblance to Leontes and Paulina's description of Leontes' baby daughter. Children are nature's miracles, and these two as welcome "as is the spring to the earth" (5.1.151). So Leontes prays that "the blessed gods" may "purge all infection from our air" whilst their stay lasts (5.1.168), a phrase harking back to the description of Delphos, intimations of a transfigured nature matching our sense of a transfigured humanity. Man is, at his royal best, almost divine:

> You have a holy father,
> A graceful gentleman; against whose person,
> So sacred as it is, I have done sin.
> For which the heavens, taking angry note
> Have left me issueless.
>
> (5.1.170)

The supreme punishment here, especially for a king, is to be left without natural issue; Florizel, however, lives, to render his father "bless'd" (5.1.174). Through the royalistic convention the poetry touches some truth concerning man, his high worth in the creative chain, his ultimate stature, that out-distances political concepts.

This semi-divine essence is also dependent on the creative love-faith of the young pair. Disaster dogs them. After surviving "dreadful Neptune" (5.1.154), they hear of Polixenes' pursuit. But, though "Heaven set spies" (5.1.203) on them; though the "stars," in another typical image, will first "kiss the valleys" (5.1.206) before they be united; indeed, though Fortune appear as a "visible enemy" (5.1.216), their love is to remain firm. As Leontes gazes on Perdita, the stern Paulina remarks that his eye "hath too much youth in't" (5.1.225), and reminds him of Hermione. "I thought of her," he answers, softly, "even in these looks I made" (5.1.227).

Leontes' reunion with his daughter is presented indirectly by the gentlemen's conversation: it has already been dramatized in *Pericles* and our present dramatic emphasis is to fall on Hermione's resurrection. These gentlemen converse in a prose of courtly formality, leaving poetry to return in full contrast later. The scene is preparatory to the greater miracle and its style well-considered, introducing us lightly and at a distance to those deep emotions which we are soon to feel with so powerful a subjective sympathy. It strikes a realistic and contemporary note, using the well-known trick of laying solid foundations before an unbelievable event: we are being habituated to impossible reunions. Moreover, the slightly ornate decorum leads on to the formal, ritualistic, quality of the later climax. There is emphasis, as one expects, on Perdita's innate and actual royalty "above her breeding" (5.2.41) and a comparison of earlier events to "an old tale" (5.2.30, 67; cp. 5.3.117). The description, plastic rather than dramatic, serves to create a *sub specie aeternitatis* effect and so to further prepare us for the statue-scene:

> They seemed almost, with staring on one another, to tear the cases of their eyes; *there was speech in their dumbness, language in their very gesture*; they looked as they had heard of *a world ransomed, or one destroyed*: a notable passion of *wonder* appeared in them; but the wisest beholder, that knew no more but seeing, could not say if the importance were *joy or sorrow*; but in the extremity of the one it must needs be.
>
> (5.2.12)

My italicized phrases are important. With the first compare the Poet's comment on a painting in *Timon of Athens*: "To the dumbness of the gesture one might interpret . . ." (1.1.34): see also *Cymbeline*, 2.4.83–85. The watchers are, to quote Milton, made "marble with too much conceiving"; made to share the frozen immobility of art. Leontes' reaction to Hermione's statue is to be similar. Next, notice the apocalyptic suggestion of "ransomed" and "destroyed": is the miracle a transfiguration of nature or wholly transcendental? Certainly it strikes "wonder." Last, observe the indecisive reference to "joy" and "sorrow," which recurs again in description of Paulina:

> But O! the noble combat that 'twixt joy and sorrow was fought in Paulina. She had one eye declined for the loss of her husband, another elevated that the oracle was fulfilled.
>
> (5.2.80)

Exactly such a blend of joy and sorrow is to characterize our final scene. Though we are pointed to "the dignity of this act" performed by kings and princes (5.2.88), it is all carried lightly, the dialogue following on with courtly fluency:

> One of the prettiest touches of all, and that which angled for mine eyes—caught the water though not the fish— was when at the relation of the queen's death, with the manner how she came to it.
>
> (5.2.91)

And yet the easy, almost bantering, manner can, without losing its identity, handle the most solemn emotions justly, as in the account of Leontes' confession:

> Who was most marble there changed colour; some swounded, all sorrowed; if all the world could have seen it, the woe had been universal.
>
> (5.1.100)

As in "ransom'd" and "redeem'd" earlier, the drama is, as it were, on the edge of something "universal": we watch more than a particular incident.

Now this dialogue has been leading us on very carefully to its own little climax, directly preparatory to the play's conclusion:

> No; the princess hearing of her mother's statue, which is in the keeping of Paulina—a piece many years in doing, and now newly performed by that rare Italian master, Julio Romano; who, had he himself *eternity* and could put *breath* into his work, would beguile *Nature* of her custom, so perfectly he is her ape: he so near to Hermione hath done Hermione that they say one would speak to her and stand in hope of answer: thither with all greediness of affection are they gone, and there they intend to sup.
>
> (5.2.105)

For the general thought of art imitating nature's human handiwork, compare the "nature's journeymen" of Hamlet's address to the Players (*Hamlet* 3.2.38). Here the statue is already associated with "eternity," regarded as the creative origin; "breath" is to be important again. The implications of "eternity" are semi-transcendental in attempt to define that unmotivated power behind the mystery of free generation in nature and in art; indeed, implicit in freedom itself. The Gentlemen next refer to the statue as "some great matter" already suspected from Paulina's continual visits to the "removed house" where it stands (5.2.117–20). We are made thoroughly expectant, attuned to a consciousness where "every wink of an eye some new grace will be born" (5.2.124); a queer phrase whose courtly ease points the miracle of creation in time—there was a mysticism within Renaissance of courtliness, as Castiglione's book indicates—whilst recalling the apocalyptic phrase in the New Testament about men being changed "in the twinkling of an eye."

Both through Paulina's dialogue with Leontes in 5.1 and the Gentlemen's conversation we have been prepared for the resurrection. But there are earlier hints, not yet observed. At Hermione's death, Paulina asserted:

> If you can bring
> Tincture or lustre in her lip, her eye,
> *Heat outwardly or breath within*, I'll serve you
> As I would do the gods.
>
> (3.2.205)

A warm physical realism is regularly here felt as essential to resurrection. Paulina is suggesting that it would need a Cerimon, in Christian thought Christ, to work the miracle: the possibility at least was thus early suggested. Later Florizel referred to just such superhuman power when, after calling vast nature and all men as witness, he swore:

> That, were I crown'd the most imperial monarch,
> Thereof most worthy, were I the fairest youth
> That ever made eye swerve, *had force and knowledge
> More than was ever man's*, I would not prize them
> Without her love.
>
> (4.3.385)

This close association of royalty ("crowned," "imperial," "monarch") with superhuman strength and wisdom may assist our interpretations elsewhere of Shakespeare's later royalism, whose spirituality (too use a dangerously ambiguous word) was forecast in Romeo's and Cleopatra's dreams of immortal, and therefore *imperial*, love (*Romeo and Juliet* 5.1.9; *Antony and Cleopatra* 5.2.76–100). The king is, at the limit, a concept of superman status. Florizel later addresses Camillo in similar style:

> How, Camillo,
> May this, almost a miracle, be done?
> That I may call thee something more than man,
> And after that trust to thee.
>
> (4.3.546)

Another clear reminiscence of Cerimon, with suggestions of some greater than human magic; white magic.

Now, as the resurrection draws near, we are prepared for it by Perdita's restoration. St. Paul once seems, perhaps justly, to consider resurrection as no more remarkable than birth (see Romans 4:17 in Dr. Moffatt's translation). Certainly here the safeguarding of Perdita is considered scarcely less wonderful than the resurrection of the dead. That the child should be found, says Paulina,

> Is all as monstrous to our *human reason*
> As my Antigonus to break his grave
> And come again to me.
>
> (5.1.41)

Yet she is restored, as the Gentlemen recount, and human reason accordingly negated. Scattered throughout are dim foreshadowings of the miraculous. Nevertheless, death looms large enough still, in poetry's despite: Paulina sees to that. When a gentleman praises Perdita she remarks:

> O Hermione!
> As every present time doth boast itself
> Above a better gone, so must thy grave
> Give way to what's seen now.
>
> (5.1.95)

The temporal order demands that the past slip away, that it lose reality; the more visible present always seems *superior*. Paulina resents this; and her remark may be aligned with both our early lines on boyhood never dreaming of any future other than to be "boy eternal" (1.2.65) and Florizel's desire to have Perdita's every act in turn—speaking, dancing, etc.—perpetuated. All these are strivings after eternity. Paulina, moreover, here suggests that the gentleman concerned, who seems to be a poet, is himself at fault: his verse, which "flow'd with her (i.e., Hermione's) beauty once," is now "shrewdly ebb'd" (5.1.102). The complaint is, not that Hermione has gone, but that the gentleman has failed in some sense to keep level. Death is accordingly less an objective reality than a failure of the subject to keep abreast of life. This may seem to turn an obvious thought into meaningless metaphysics, but the lines, in their context, can scarcely be ignored. Throughout *Troilus and Cressida* (especially at 3.3.145–84, an expansion of Paulina's comment) Shakespeare's thoughts on time are highly abstruse (see my essay in *The Wheel of Fire*); so are they in the Sonnets. Wrongly used time is as intrinsic to the structure of *Macbeth* as is "eternity" to that of *Antony and Cleopatra* (see my essays on both plays in *The Imperial Theme*). As so often in great poetry, the philosophical subtlety exists within or behind a speech, or plot, of surface realism and simplicity. Now *The Winter's Tale* is hammering on the threshold of some extraordinary truth related to both "nature" and "eternity." Hence its emphasis on the seasons, birth and childhood, the continual moulding of new miracles on the pattern of the old; hence, too, the desire expressed for youthful excellent perpetuated and eternal; the thought of Perdita's every action as a "crowned" thing, a "queen," in its own eternal right (4.3.145–46); and also of art as improving or distorting nature, in the flower-dialogue, in Julio Romano's uncanny, eternity-imitating, skill. And yet no metaphysics, no natural philosophy or art, satisfy the demand that the lost thing, in all its nature-born warmth, be preserved; that it, not only its descendant, shall live; that death be revealed as a sin-born illusion; that eternity be flesh and blood.

The action moves to the house of the "grave and good Paulina" (5.3.1). The scene is her "chapel," recalling the chapel of death at 3.2.240, where Leontes last saw Hermione's dead body. Paulina shows them the statue, which excels anything "the hand of man hath done" (5.3.17); and they are quickly struck with—again the word—"wonder" (5.2.22). Leontes gazes; recognizes Hermione's "natural posture" (5.3.23); asks her to chide him, yet remembers how she was tender "as infancy and grace" (5.3.27):

> O! thus she stood,
> Even with such life of majesty—warm life
> As now it coldly stands—when first I woo'd her.
> I am asham'd: does not the stone rebuke me
> For being more stone than it? O, royal piece!
>
> (5.3.34)

Sweet though it be, it remains cold and withdrawn, like Keats's
Grecian Urn. Yet its "majesty" exerts a strangely potent "magic"
(5.3.39) before which Perdita kneels almost in "superstition" (5.3.43).
Leontes' grief is so great that Camillo reminds him how "sixteen
winters" and "so many summers" should by now alternately have
blown and dried his soul clean of "sorrow"; why should that prove
more persistent than short-lived "joy"? (5.3.49–53). Leontes remains still, his soul pierced (5.3.34) by remembrance. Paulina,
however, speaks realistically of the statue as art, saying how its
colour is not dry yet (5.3.47); half-apologizing for the way it moves
him, her phrase "for the stone is mine" (5.3.58) re-emphasizing her
peculiar office. She offers to draw the curtain, fearing lest Leontes'
"fancy may think anon it moves" (5.3.61). The excitement gener-
ated, already intense, reaches new impact and definition in Paulina's
sharp ringing utterance on "moves."

But Leontes remains quiet, fixed, in an other-worldly consciousness, a living death not to be disturbed, yet trembling with
expectance;

> Let be, let be!
> Would I were dead, but that, methinks, already—
> What was he that did make it?
>
> (5.3.61)

A universe of meaning is hinted by that one word "already" and
the subsequent, tantalizing, break. Now the statue seems no longer
cold:

> See, my lord,
> Would you not deem it breath'd, and that those veins
> Did verily bear blood?
>
> (5.3.63)

As the revelation slowly matures, it is as though Leontes' own grief
and love were gradually infusing the thing before him with life. He,

under Paulina, is labouring, even now, that it may live. The more
visionary, paradisal, personal wonder of Pericles (who alone hears
the spheral music) becomes here a crucial conflict, an *agon*, in which
many persons share; dream is being forced into actuality. "Masterly
done," answers Polixenes, taking us back to common-sense, and
yet again noting that "the very life seems warm upon her lip"
(5.3.65). We are poised between motion and stillness, life and art:

> The fixure of her eye has motion in't,
> As we are mock'd with art.
>
> (5.3.67)

The contrast drives deep, recalling the balancing of art and nature in
Perdita's dialogue with Polixenes; and, too, the imaging of the
living Marina as "crown'd Truth" or monumental Patience (*Pericles*
5.1.124, 140). Paulina reiterates her offer to draw the curtain lest
Leontes be so far "transported" (cp. 3.2.159; a word strongly toned
in Shakespeare with magical suggestion) that he actually think it
"lives"—thus recharging the scene with an impossible expectation.
To which Leontes replies:

> No settled senses of the world can match
> The pleasure of that madness. Let't alone.
>
> (5.3.72)

He would stand here, spell-bound, forever; forever gazing on this
sphinx-like boundary between art and life.

Paulina, having functioned throughout as the Oracle's imple-
ment, becomes now its priestess. Her swift changes key the scene
to an extraordinary pitch, as she hints at new marvels:

> I am sorry, sir, I have thus far stirr'd you: but
> I could afflict you further.
>
> (5.3.74)

She has long caused, and still causes, Leontes to suffer poignantly;
and yet his suffering has undergone a subtle change, for now this
very "affliction has a taste as sweet as any cordial comfort" (5.3.76).
Already (at 5.2.20 and 81, and 5.3.51–53) we have found joy and
sorrow in partnership, as, too, in the description of Cordelia's grief
(*King Lear* 4.3.17–26). So Leontes endures a pain of ineffable
sweetness as the mystery unfolds:

> Still, methinks,
> There is an air comes from her: what fine chisel
> Could ever yet cut breath?
>
> (5.3.77)

However highly we value the eternity phrased by art (as in Yeats's "monuments of unaging intellect" in *Sailing to Byzantium* and Keats's "Grecian Urn," yet there is a frontier beyond which it and all corresponding philosophies fail: they lack one thing, breath. With a fine pungency of phrase, more humanly relevant than Othello's "I know not where is that Promethean heat" (*Othello* 5.2.12), a whole world of human idealism is dismissed. The supreme moments of earlier tragedy—Othello before the "monumental alabaster" (5.2.5) of the sleeping Desdemona, Romeo in Capel's monument, Juliet and Cleopatra blending sleep and death—are implicit in Leontes' experience; more, their validity is at stake, as he murmurs, "Let no man mock me" (5.3.79), stepping forward for an embrace; as old Lear, reunited with Cordelia, "a spirit in bliss," says "Do not laugh at me" (*King Lear* 4.7.68); as Pericles fears lest his reunion with Marina be merely such a dream as "mocks" man's grief (*Pericles* 5.1.144, 164). Those, and other, supreme moments of pathos are here re-enacted to a stronger purpose. Leontes strides forward; is prevented by Paulina; we are brought up against a *cul-de-sac*. But Paulina herself immediately releases new impetus as she cries, her voice quivering with the Sibylline power she wields:

> Either forbear,
> Quit presently the chapel, or resolve you
> For more amazement. If you can behold it,
> I'll make the statue move indeed, descend,
> And take you by the hand; but then you'll think—
> Which I protest against—I am assisted
> By wicked powers.
>
> (5.3.85)

The "chapel" setting is necessary, for we attend the resurrection of a supposedly buried person; the solemnity is at least half funereal. Much is involved in the phrase "wicked powers": we watch no act of necromancy. The "magic" (5.2.39), if magic it be, is a white magic; shall we say, a natural magic; the living opposite of the Ghost in *Hamlet* hideously breaking his tomb's "ponderous and marble jaws" (1.4.50). The difference is that between Prospero's powers in *The Tempest* and those of Marlowe's Faustus or of the Weird Sisters in *Macbeth*. The distinction in Shakespeare's day was important and further driven home by Paulina's:

> It is requir'd
> You do awake your faith. Then, all stand still;
> Or those that think it is unlawful business
> I am about, let them depart.
>
> (5.3.94)

The key-word "faith" enlists New Testament associations, but to it Paulina adds a potency more purely Shakespearian: music. Shakespeare's use of music, throughout his main antagonist to tempestuous tragedy, reaches a newly urgent precision at Cerimon's restoration of Thaisa and Pericles' reunion with Marina. Here it functions strongly as the specifically releasing agent:

> PAULINA: Music, awake her: strike!
> 'Tis time; descend; be stone no more; approach;
> Strike all that look upon with marvel. Come;
> I'll fill your grave up: stir, nay, come away;
> Bequeath to death your numbness, for from him
> Dear life redeems you. You perceive she stirs.
> Start not; her actions shall be holy as
> You hear my spell is lawful: do not shun her
> Until you see her die again, for then
> You kill her double. Nay, present your hand:
> When she was young you woo'd her; now in age
> Is she become the suitor?
> LEONTES: O! she's warm.
> If this be magic, let it be an art
> Lawful as eating.
>
> (5.3.98)

"Redeems" (cp. "ransomed" at 5.2.16), "holy" and "lawful" continue earlier emphases. The concreteness of "fill your grave up" has analogies in Shelley's *Witch of Atlas* (69–71) and the empty sepulchre of the New Testament. Such resurrections are imaged as a re-infusing of the dead body with life. Hermione's restoration not only has nothing to do with black magic; it is not even transcendental. It exists in warm human actuality (cp. *Pericles* 5.1.154): hence our earlier emphases on warmth and breath; and now on "eating" too. It is, indeed, part after all of "great creating nature"; no more, and no less; merely another miracle from the great power, the master-artist of creation, call it what you will, nature or eternity, Apollo or—as in the New Testament—"the living God."

The poet carefully refuses to elucidate the mystery on the plane of plot-realism. When Polixenes wonders where Hermione "has liv'd" or "how stol'n from the dead," Paulina merely observes that she *is* living, and that this truth, if reported rather than experienced, would "be hooted at like an old tale" (5.3.114–17; cp. "like an old tale" at 5.2.30, 67). Perdita's assistance is needed to unloose Hermione's speech; whereupon she speaks, invoking the gods' "sacred vials" of blessing on her daughter and referring to the Oracle (5.3.121–28). Leontes further drives home our enigma by remarking that Paulina has found his wife, though "how is to be question'd"; for, he says,

> I saw her
> As I thought, dead, and have in vain said many
> A prayer upon her grave.
>
> (5.3.139)

We are not, in fact, to search for answers on this plane at all: the poet himself does not know them. Certainly our plot-realism is maintained: Paulina reminds us that her husband is gone; and we may remember Mamillius. It is the same in *Pericles*. The subsidiary persons are no longer, as persons, important: the perfunctory marrying of Paulina and Camillo to round off the ritual might otherwise be a serious blemish.

The truth shadowed, or revealed, is only to be known, if at all, within the subjective personality, the "I" not easily linked into an objective argument. It is precisely this mysterious "I" in the audience that the more important persons of drama, and in especial tragedy, regularly objectify. Now within the "I" rest all those undefinables and irrationalities of free-will and guilt, of unconditioned and therefore appallingly responsible action with which *The Winter's Tale* is throughout deeply concerned; as in Leontes' unmotivated sin for which he is nevertheless in some sense responsible; with his following loss of free-will, selling himself in bondage to dark powers, and a consequent enduring and infliction of tyranny. The outward effects are suspicion, knowledge of evil and violent blame; with a final spreading and miserable knowledge of death ("There was a man dwelt by a churchyard"—2.1.28), leading on, with Paulina's assistance, to repentance. Time is throughout present as a backward-flowing thing, swallowing and engulfing; we are sunk deep in the consciousness of dead facts, causes, death. But over against all this stands the creative consciousness, existing not in present-past but present-future, and with a sense of causation not behind but ahead, the ever-flowing in of the new and uncondi-tioned, from future to present: this is the consciousness of freedom, in which "every wink of an eye some new grace will be born" (5.2.124). Hence our poetry plays queer tricks with time, as in the "boy eternal" passage where consciousness is confined to "to-day" and "to-morrow": in Florizel's dreams of immediate perfection eternalized; in thought of "eternity" (which includes the future, being over-dimensional to the time-stream) as the creative origin; and in Paulina's annoyance at the poet-gentleman's ready submis-sion to time the destroyer. Freedom is creation, and therefore art; and hence our emphases on art, in the flower-dialogue, in notice of Julio Romano's skill, in the statue-scene; and here we approach a vital problem. It is precisely the creative spirit in man, the unmoti-vated and forward "I," that binds him to "great creating Nature," the "great nature" by whose laws the child is "freed and enfran-chised" from the womb (2.2.60–61): he is one with that nature, in so far as he is free. Our drama works therefore to show Leontes, under the tutelage of the Oracle, as painfully working himself from the bondage of sin and remorse into the freedom of nature, with the aptly-named Paulina as conscience, guide, and priestess. The resur-rection is not performed until (1) Leontes' repentance is complete and (2) creation is satisfied by the return of Perdita, who is needed for Hermione's full release. Religion, art, procreation, and nature (in "warmth," "breath" and "eating") are all contributory to the conclusion, which is shown as no easy release, but rather a gradual revelation, corresponding to Pericles' reunion with Marina, under terrific dramatic pressure and fraught with an excitement with which the watcher's "I" is, by most careful technique, forced into a close subjective identity, so that the immortality revealed is less concept than experience. Nor is it just a reversal of tragedy; rather tragedy is contained, assimilated, transmuted; every phrase of the resurrection scene is soaked in tragic feeling, and the accompanying joy less an antithesis to sorrow than its final flowering. The depths of the "I," which are tragic, are being integrated with the objective delight which is nature's joy. The philosophy of Wordsworth is forecast; for he, too, knew Leontes' abysmal "nothing"; he too suffered some hideous disillusion, in part evil; he too laboured slowly for reintegration with nature; and, finally, he too saw man's true state in terms of creation and miracle. The response, in both Wordsworth and Shakespeare, is a reverential wonder at knowledge of Life where Death was throned.

The Winter's Tale may seem a rambling, perhaps an untidy, play; its anachronisms are vivid, its geography disturbing. And yet Shakespeare offers nothing greater in tragic psychology, humour, pastoral, romance, and that which tops them all and is, except for *Pericles*, new. The unity of thought is more exact than appears: it was Sicily, at first sight ill-suited to the sombre scenes here staged, that gave us the myth of Proserpine or Persephone. The more profound passages are perhaps rather evidence of what is beating behind or within the creative genius at work than wholly successful ways of printing purpose on an average audience's, or an average reader's, mind; but the passages are there, and so is the purpose, though to Shakespeare it need not have been defined outside his drama. That drama, however, by its very enigma, its unsolved and yet uncompromising statement, throws up—as in small compass did the little flower-dialogue too—a vague, numinous, sense of mighty powers, working through both the natural order and man's religious consciousness, that preserve, in spite of all appearance, the good. Orthodox tradition is used, but it does not direct; a pagan naturalism is used too. The Bible has been an influence; so have classical myth and Renaissance pastoral; but the greatest influence was Life itself, that creating and protecting deity whose superhuman presence and powers the drama labours to define.

"But It Appears She Lives": Iteration in *The Winter's Tale*

James Edward Siemon

The plot of *The Winter's Tale* gives form to an acute assessment of the potential for good and for evil in a social world. As we see them in the play, both good and evil are possibilities inherent in the human condition, and the dominance of good at the end of the play is neither complete nor absolute: the devastation wrought by Leontes' jealousy cannot be forgotten, and the joy arising from the love of Perdita and Florizel, though real and important, is limited.

In its structural pattern the play undoubtedly draws upon a ritual movement, characteristic of the romantic comedies, which has been well described as a movement "from release to clarification" or as a withdrawal from a comic world of inhibiting social conventions to a more primitive world in which human emotions are allowed freer scope. But despite the central importance of the Bohemia scenes to the meaning of the play, Shakespeare gives the greatest attention to Leontes' court and puts it at the center of the emphatic opening and closing scenes. The court is an emblem of the world, and the ritual action of the play takes the form of a withdrawal from the world followed by a return to it. From another point of view, however, the ritual action of the play is iterative as well as serial, thus creating a double withdrawal: first, a withdrawal from the sterile social world of Leontes' court to the fecund world of pastoral Bohemia; and second, a withdrawal from the sterile world of Polixenes' court mores to a Sicilian court that now has at its center not Leontes' destructive mania but Paulina's creative magic.

From *PMLA* 89, no. 1 (January 1974). © 1974 by the Modern Language Association of America.

What I wish to do here is to suggest the extent and importance of iteration in *The Winter's Tale*. For the second part of the play, while completing the first, stands also (I believe) as an alternative to it, parallel but distinct in its action. And it is from variant repetition of common motifs in the two parts of the play that we come to see good and evil as exercising mutual restraints upon one another.

I

The play is drawn together by repeated insistence upon the ambiguities of appearance. Hence the multiple and comic ironies of Perdita's debate with Polixenes in 4.4. A shepherdess who intends at the first opportunity to wed a prince argues vehemently against "nature's bastards"; a king who will oppose with all of the power at his command a prince's marriage to a shepherdess argues gracefully for making "conceive a bark of baser kind / By bud of nobler race." The debate is finally inconclusive. Polixenes' civilized theories are never brought to the test (although his commitment to them is exposed as sham), and by the revelation of her true identity, Perdita is saved from facing the implications of her purist doctrine for a shepherdess in love with a prince.

But the debate is properly felt to lie near the core of the play not only because it states theories of value that effect action in the play, but because it dramatizes the great difficulty each major character experiences in his attempts to translate theory into action. Polixenes acts more on Perdita's theory than on his own, and Perdita's actions are consistent with her own theory only as an expression of some deeply and powerfully felt sense of her own nobility. The comedy of the debate is thus far-reaching, and Perdita's puritanical disgust at nature's bastards is genuinely amusing. But the issues, and even, to some extent, the dramatic situation, have been anticipated in the conflict between Leontes and Hermione.

Both Nevill Coghill and William Matchett have emphasized the extensive ambivalence that surrounds Hermione in the first act. She makes her initial appearance in a state of advanced pregnancy to the accompaniment of a detailed insistence upon Polixenes' nine months' residence in Sicilia and sets about a verbal exchange with Polixenes that is laden with sexual innuendo. It is not until the oracle is read that the fact of Hermione's chastity is unequivocally stated. Of course, one has long since accepted Hermione's account of herself. It is amply supported by her dignity and self-assurance in the face of Leontes' attack upon her, and it is reinforced by the sympathetic support given her by all of the right-thinking courtiers. Yet even Antigonus is prepared to accept Leontes' charges, as his reaction to this shipboard vision makes clear (see 3.3.41–46). The initial action of the play calls into question neither Leontes' theory about the proper behavior of a queen nor his theory about the proper punishment of a queen who misbehaves. Rather, it calls into question his easy conviction that simple theory can be translated directly into simple action. And this is a point on which Perdita's debate with Polixenes turns. Perdita herself, according to Leontes, is one of nature's bastards, and he will no more have her in his court than she will have "streak'd gillyvors" in her garden. Even the strain of rigid cruelty with which Leontes holds to his theory is repeated (in a lower key, of course) in Perdita's contemptuous assertion that "I'll not put / The dibble in earth to set one slip of them" (4.4.99–100), and, in its original key, in the fury with which Polixenes turns on Perdita (4.4.423–42). If anything, the action of the play vindicates both Leontes' and Perdita's purist theories; what it condemns is any attempt to act upon those theories without regard to the ambiguities of appearance and the complexities of reality.

Life as it is depicted in the play is a thing of wonder, constantly betraying the neat theories of men. The characters' sense of wonder mounts continuously until the fifth act, where possibilities about to be realized are proclaimed "monstrous to human reason"; events "will bear no credit, / Were not the proof so nigh"; revelations evoke "amazedness," "a notable passion of wonder," "a deal of wonder." The truth is, as Leontes finally remarks, beyond comprehension: "Thou hast found mine; / But how, is to be question'd; for I saw her, / As I thought, dead" (5.3.138–40).

But like the difficulties that Perdita and Polixenes experience in translating theory into action, wonder and incomprehension at the inexplicable turn of events have been anticipated in the first part of the play. Despite critical efforts to provide for Leontes' jealous outburst through judicious staging or to anticipate it in his deportment from his first appearance, the jealousy seems to be instantaneous in its birth and immediately poisonous in its effects. Probably, as William Matchett argues in his impressive analysis of act 1, scene 2, the audience should expect Leontes to act more or less as he does;

but to his court, his actions are inexplicable, as the characters surrounding him repeatedly tell us. Hermione's reaction as she grasps the implications of his jealous rage—stunned disbelief yielding to wonder—is precisely Leontes' when she steps down from her pedestal. These are things to be wondered at. We are invited by the play to accept what comes about rather than to inquire too closely into the means by which it comes. Paulina probably has, as so often, the last word:

> That she is living,
> Were it but told you, should be hooted at
> Like an old tale: but it appears she lives
> (5.3.115–17)

Insistence upon the unreliability of appearance is continuous from Hermione's entrance until she steps down from her pedestal. It is, therefore, a continuing source of dramatic irony, which in the first part of the play is centered principally on the question of Hermione's chastity, but in the fourth and fifth acts centers upon Perdita's natural nobility. To Florizel,

> Each your doing,
> So singular in each particular,
> Crowns what you are doing, in the present deeds,
> That all your acts are queens.
> (4.4.143–46)

And to Polixenes,

> This is the prettiest low-born lass that ever
> Ran on the green-sward: nothing she does or seems
> But smacks of something greater than herself,
> Too noble for this place.
> (4.4.156–59)

Such irony reaches its climax when Leontes, confronted with Florizel and his unknown princess, recalls the lost Mamillius and Perdita:

> I lost a couple, that 'twixt heaven and earth
> Might thus have stood, begetting wonder, as
> You, gracious couple, do
> (5.1.131–33)

> What might I have been,
> Might I a son and daughter now have look'd on,
> Such goodly things as you!
>
> (5.1.175–77)

Florizel is to be Leontes' son, just as, in his equivocation, Florizel has insisted that his shepherdess will be the daughter of a king "When once she is my wife." And Leontes is, in part, to be what he might have been. For Florizel also occupies Mamillius's place in the pattern of loss and recovery as a son restored to a father, a place suggested in the ambiguous language of Camillo's vision:

> Methinks I see
> Leontes opening his free arms and weeping
> His welcome forth; asks thee there "Son, forgiveness!"
> As 'twere i'th'father's person
>
> (4.4.548–51)

Leontes is in the father's person, and the language cannot be other than intentional.

In their union, Florizel and Perdita complete the customary comic pattern of true love impeded but brought to fruition. In this, they stand as surrogates to Leontes and Hermione, completing a pattern which Leontes' madness has shattered; but they are also alternatives to Leontes and Hermione, a new generation representing anew the possibilities inherent in love and in a healthy community. And through the new generation, these possibilities are in a measure restored to the older generation. It is through Perdita, the extension in time of his own flesh, that Leontes is reunited with Hermione. Just as Perdita's time of exile corresponds to Leontes' time of mourning, so her growth and nurture in the semipastoral world of Bohemia provides a parallel in the action of the play to her father's spiritual rebirth and growth, and she comes to represent both his flesh and his spirit. The restoration to Leontes of these extensions of his own being, his wife and child, is at once cause and effect in his own redemption.

The revelation of Perdita's true identity and the restoration of Hermione are actions of parallel consequence and meaning: the relegation of the one to offstage business (presumably in order to avoid anticlimax) suggests that they are of potentially equivalent dramatic force. Each is the culmination of a pattern extending throughout the play in which goodness is mistaken, discarded, and laboriously recovered. This pattern of loss and recovery requires complications of the sort that attend Hermione's trial and Florizel's courtship, and ritual of the sort that attends the sending to the oracle for its pronouncements or of the sort devised by Paulina when she makes her lawful spell. What has been lost has been lost through the actions of men, and what is to be won must be won from the gods. Loss has come through trusting too readily to appearance, and recovery is accompanied by insistence that there is a truth which lies behind appearance and which men ignore at their peril. The statue scene is only the most theatrical of the scenes that dramatize the complex and elusive nature of reality.

II

Repeated insistence upon the ambiguities of appearance, upon the dangers inherent in any attempt to subject those ambiguities to simple analysis, and upon the need to accept the truth as complex and even at times beyond comprehension thus contributes to our sense that in the complicated plot of The Winter's Tale there is a cohesive and continuous single action. At the same time, many of the details that contribute to this sense of cohesion also work within a larger pattern of structural repetition that serves to make the action of the second half of the play independent from as well as continuous upon that of the first. Camillo's role in each half of the play casts a clear light on this aspect of their relation. In the first, he appears as the trusted adviser to a king; betrays his king; flees the kingdom; is dramatically vindicated in the revelation of an oracle. In the second, he appears as the trusted adviser to a king; betrays his king; hastily leaves the kingdom; is dramatically vindicated in the providential revelation of Perdita's identity.

We are assured by the testimony of the two kings and by the outcome of events that Camillo is a wise and deserving man. Were we to judge him by his actions alone, we might reach a different conclusion, for we see him as a schemer and as an accomplished equivocator. Camillo's dramatic ancestor is no doubt that wily slave of classical comedy whose devious schemes are the efficient cause of the comic resolution. In The Winter's Tale, he has something of this role, for his trickiness is instrumental in effecting the resolution of each half of the play, although he is not alone the efficient cause of either resolution. Insofar as Camillo's role goes, the second half of the play is little more than the first half all over again. His character is skillfully worked into his role, so that his honorable distaste for killing kings leads him to betray Leontes, and his love for Leontes (and, apparently, his wish to help Florizel) leads him to betray Polixenes. His role, however, is itself determined by the demands of the comic pattern as it is worked out in the play's recurrent plot motifs.

But it is not only in Camillo's role that the play repeats itself. The distance might seem great between accusing a queen of adultery with a king and accusing a milkmaid of seducing a prince. Upon close analysis that distance narrows. There is present in both charges a sexual issue and an emphasis upon physical detail: Hermione is a "hobby-horse, deserves a name / As rank as any flax-wench that puts to / Before her trothplight" (1.2.276–78); Perdita is a "fresh piece / Of excellent witchcraft," an "enchantment" who would open "rural latches" to Florizel's entrance and "hoop his body" in her embraces (4.4.423–42, et passim). Polixenes' sudden discovery of himself in the midst of the sheep-shearing feast reproduces the motif of Leontes' sudden madness in the midst of a scene of courtly compliment. There are, too, interesting recurrences of psychological detail. Some of the force behind Leontes' wrath comes from his sense of betrayal:

> as he does conceive
> He is dishonour'd by a man which ever
> Profess'd to him; why, his revenges must
> In that be made more bitter.
> (1.2.454–57)

This same motif recurs in 4.4, where a part of Polixenes' outrage clearly arises from his sense that Florizel has betrayed him. Again, in Perdita's calm response to Polixenes' tirade.

> I was not much afeard; for once or twice
> I was about to speak, and tell him plainly,
> The selfsame sun that shines upon his court
> Hides not his visage from our cottage, but
> Looks on alike.
> (4.4.443–47)

there sounds a clear echo of Hermione's clear-sighted courage.

The parallel does not extend to every detail, but its force shows even in quite small details. It cannot be chance that twice in this play a princess of Sicilia is accused of sexual irregularity with a prince of Bohemia. Each of the two halves of the play has a wrathful king; innocent victims; a princess slandered; a servant who serves his master's highest interests by betraying him; a kingdom without an heir or threatened with the loss of its heir; a voyage over a stormy sea; a providential revelation. There are confusions of identity present from the first. In the early scenes these take the form of mistaking things for what they are not—to Polixenes, Hermione, and Camillo, Leontes seems a loving and trusting husband; to Leontes, Hermione seems an adulteress, Camillo a traitor, Perdita a bastard, and he himself a cuckold. The motif is repeated in the second half of the play, where Perdita is taken for a shepherdess, Florizel for a swain, Polixenes and Camillo for benign visitors, Autolycus for an honest man. But the motif is also reversed in the second half, so that things which are not what they appear to be are instinctively recognized for what they really are: Perdita a princess; Perdita and Florizel Leontes' children. The kings are by courtesy, as well as in temperament and in their slightly morbid concern with the details of sexuality, brothers; the wronged princesses are mother and daughter. Each part has at its center two men and a woman: two "brothers" and a queen of Sicilia; father and son and a princess of Sicilia. There can be little doubt that the second part of the play represents a conscious variation on the themes and plot motifs of the first.

Hermione's loss and recovery is at once the central problem in the relation of the two parts of the play and the clearest indication that we may see its two-part structure as giving form to a concept of independent possibilities. It has long been noticed that the details surrounding her death are not in accord with some that accompany her reappearance. It is possible to account for this discrepancy by positing an earlier version of the play whose final scene was in line with *Pandosto*, and a careless revision which neglected particularly the details of act 3, scene 2. It is equally possible to account for the discrepancy by a theory of dramatic sleight-of-hand designed to give the fullest effectiveness to the statue scene. But although there is precedent for Shakespeare's occasional inattention to detail, the details attending Hermione's death are too important for one to suppose that they could pass unnoticed in a revision. Yet, to treat the statue scene as only a coup de theatre is to reduce to parlor-trick mummery in deplorable taste the solemn music and ritual with which Paulina invokes Hermione to "descend; be stone no more; approach . . . Bequeath to death your numbness; for from him / Dear life redeems you," and this is simply not the effect of the scene. A third possibility is to accept both act 3, scene 2, and act 5, scene 3, at their full dramatic value.

The inexplicable bounty of Hermione's restoration is prepared for in act 3, scene 2, a scene whose conclusion one cannot read without feeling the power behind Paulina's denunciation of Leontes and sensing in her speech a failure of control. Elsewhere, though outspoken, Paulina recognizes some limits; here, she speaks without restraint:

> What studied torments, tyrant, hast for me?
> What wheels? racks? fires? what flaying? boiling?
> In leads or oils? What old or newer torture
> Must I receive, whose every word deserves
> To taste of thy most worst? Thy tyranny,
> Together working with thy jealousies
> (Fancies too weak for boys, too green and idle
> For girls of nine), O think what they have done,
> And then run mad indeed: stark mad!
> (3.2.175–83)

For the first time, Paulina is rebuked by a fellow courtier for the freedom of her speech.

The dramatic effect of this outburst is to suggest that, under the pressure of grief too great to be borne, Paulina has momentarily broken down. She quickly recovers her self-control, but there is nothing to suggest that she has been dissembling. The emotional force of her outburst can only be taken to mean that Hermione is dead and that Paulina knows it. Further, in response to the court's stunned disbelief, Paulina insists that anyone in doubt may view Hermione's body: "If word nor oath / Prevail not, go and see." Were her grief a pretense designed to cover plans to spirit Hermione into hiding, this would be a bold stroke indeed. But, in fact, Leontes, accompanied apparently by the entire court, does go and see: "Prithee, bring me / To the dead bodies of my queen and son" (cf. 5.3.139–40: "for I saw her, / As I thought, dead"). And the scene immediately following (3.3) emphasizes the dramatic fact of Hermione's death:

> Come, poor babe:
> I have heard, but not believ'd, the spirits o'th'dead
> May walk again: if such thing be, thy mother
> Appear'd to me last night
>
> (3.3.15–18)

Dreams such as Antigonus's are conventional in Shakespearean drama, and the conventions vary little from the early plays (cf. Clarence's dream in *Richard III* 1.4, or Richard's own dream in 5.3) to the later plays (cf. Posthumus's dream in *Cymbeline* 5.4). It is invariably true of such dreams that the ghosts who appear in them are ghosts of the dead. Shakespeare would have been entirely free to grant Antigonus a dream vision of Apollo, as Pericles is granted a dream vision of Diana (*Pericles* 5.1), had he wished only to account for Antigonus's decision to deposit Perdita on the shores of Bohemia. That, instead, he chose to give Antigonus a vision of Hermione's ghost can only mean that he intended to reinforce the audience's belief in her death. There can be no doubt that Hermione is, at this point in the play, dead.

Against the dramatic impact of this scene, and of the statue scene itself, there stand only the Second Gentleman's remark that Paulina has "privately twice or thrice a day, ever since the death of Hermione, visited that removed house" (5.2.105–7—but since Hermione is still apparently dead, how much force can these words have?), and Hermione's cryptic promise to Perdita that "thou shalt hear that I, / Knowing by Paulina that the oracle / Gave hope thou wast in being, have preserved / Myself to see the issue" (5.3.125–28). Hermione's death is given dramatic force in Paulina's grief and rage, in Antigonus's dream, in Leontes' "saint-like sorrow," and in his stunned silence when Hermione steps down from the pedestal. That she has been alive all along is suggested only in one, or perhaps two, expository details. The details cannot be ignored altogether; they are there. But when the dramatic effect of two important scenes is at odds with the apparent meaning of minor expository details, it is not the expository details that should be dominant. The dramatic facts are that Hermione is truly dead at the end of the first part of the play and that she has returned to life at the end of the second.

Only in a reductive reading of the play (or in one that is stringently realistic) need such apparent contradiction be troubling, for Hermione's death has symbolic as well as dramatic force. The immortality that Leontes might enjoy through his children is lost to him when they are lost; the hope for such immortality is forfeited when Hermione dies. It is thus not only Hermione who dies and comes to life again. If her role in the play derives, as we are sometimes told, from the myth of Persephone, Leontes takes his part in the mythic action by spending her absence in mourning. When Hermione is restored to Leontes, something irrevocably lost is miraculously restored. But, for our sense of providential munificence to be complete, our experience of irrevocable loss must also be real. Hermione's restoration is a gift of the gods, even though men must through their actions earn such gifts, and the events surrounding her loss and recovery have a felt propriety about them as necessary and fitting details in a large and satisfactory design. To observe that they could not have taken place, or to insist that in fact they did not take place, is to ignore the design and the carefully articulated and self-conscious artifice of the play. As Clifford Leech observes of the fable of *The Winter's Tale*, "This is not life as we know it, we are again and again assured, though it may have the authority that comes from ancient tale-telling or current ceremonial. It is an emblem, not a replica." Within the emblem of the play, Hermione's death and her return from death to life are consistent and harmonious because they give the fullest dramatic value to the possibilities for loss and for gain which the action of the play provides.

III

The structure of the play thus serves to embody two aspects of a single conception of human nature and human society; its distinct but parallel actions enable Shakespeare to explore the possibilities for good and evil in society by balancing against one another variations on a single theme. The first half of the play introduces an image of community in Leontes' role as king and in his marriage to Hermione, and shows the community made sterile on every level through a mistaking of the appearance of truth for truth itself. The second half of the play reintroduces an image of community in the sheep-shearing feast, in Florizel's role as heir to a kingdom, and in the love between Florizel and Perdita. Once again there is a threat to the health of the community through a mistaking of true value: the admirable Shepherd threatened with death, the kingdom with the loss of its heir, the lovers with separation. This time it shows triumph rather than defeat. The technique is akin to the device of telling the same story from the points of view of several different characters, so that each version of the story comes to reflect one aspect of a larger truth. Here, the basic pattern of the tale recurs in each telling; it is filled out with different characters (who are, however, frequently identified with their counterparts); and the details peculiar to each version of the tale reflect potentialities inherent in all men. So, the disasters that take their terrible toll in the first telling of the tale threaten, but are averted, in the second. Hermione and Mamillius die, Perdita is denied by her father and thrust out of his life; but Perdita and Florizel do not lose one another, and despite Polixenes' threat to "not hold thee of our blood, no, not our kin," Florizel is not denied or lost to the kingdom.

It is principally negative possibilities that are given form in the first telling of the tale, positive possibilities in the second. But the values and dangers of each extend into the other, and neither can be completed without bringing the other to completion. That Florizel and Perdita keep their values straight would not be enough were either Leontes or Polixenes wholly corrupt. In the end, each part of the play defines the possibilities within the other for good and for evil. Evil is real, but it is not absolute, and there is more to life than it can encompass. Leontes can live on, however painfully, as Othello could not. On the other hand, there is goodness, and it too is not absolute, nor can it define all the possibilities of life. The joy of Hermione's recovery is inseparable from the pain of her loss, as even at this joyous moment Paulina reminds Leontes:

> Do not shun her
> Until you see her die again; for then
> You kill her double.

"Integration" in
The Winter's Tale

L. C. Knights

There is a good deal of rashness in a layman's speaking even to an "applied" section of the British Psychoanalytical Society. I have no more than a layman's and an ex-patient's knowledge of psychoanalysis and psychiatry, and I certainly shall not attempt a psychoanalytic account of the play that is my subject. Not only am I not equipped to do so, but I confess to a certain prejudice regarding attempts to apply psychoanalytical concepts to works of art. In such cases the literary critic who is not trained as an analyst can only rely on tools that have been shaped for him by others, which he may not know how to handle. The analyst who is not prepared to meet a work of art on its own terms before he applies what is essentially a clinical method may throw off some interesting observations, but he certainly runs the danger of forcing an abundant stream through the narrow channel that works his mill or—without metaphor—of imposing an interpretation that does not interpret. I think Ella Freeman Sharpe in her well-known essay "From *King Lear* to *The Tempest*" does this when she sees Lear's unruly knights as the baby's uncontrolled feces, or Lear's wandering on the heath as the emergence of an entirely supposititious event in Shakespeare's childhood. The essay does indeed remind us that the play *King Lear* reaches down to submerged layers of our consciousness—where, for example, we retain the first impact of rivalry with brothers or sisters, or a sense of early ambivalent relations between child and

---

From *The Sewanee Review* 84 (Fall 1976). © 1976 by the University of the South.

parent. But we might hope to attain these insights without such a drastic reduction of a masterwork of the philosophic imagination.

I do not of course mean that psychoanalytic and literary interests should be kept in separate compartments of our minds. The interpretation of literature demands a great variety of skills, and there is no reason why knowledge gained in clinical practice or in reading the work of psychiatrists should not enter into the reading of literature. The critical essays of D. W. Harding, for example, are the product of a fine *literary* sense; but clearly Harding could not have written as he has on, say, the guilt of Coleridge's Ancient Mariner, or on what he calls the hinterland of articulate thought, without a close acquaintance with psychology, including the psychoanalytic field. (See *Experience into Words.*) Conversely Freud's admiration—and I mean professional admiration—for Shakespeare and for Dostoevsky is well known. Recently I have noticed that D. W. Winnicott uses *Hamlet* to illustrate a theory about the balance of boy and girl elements in boy or girl—and does it in a way that (to me at all events) throws back light on the play itself. Perhaps a literary critic may take heart from Ernst Kris's remark that, at all events "in marginal areas," "there are problems of research which might be presented in better perspective were the testimony of the literary mind to be taken fully into account." Perhaps, however, the areas are not necessarily marginal.

No doubt others with a wider range than my own could produce very many examples of fruitful interplay between these two different fields of knowledge. My point is a very simple one: namely that useful insights are most likely to emerge when thought is allowed to *play* between them: there must be no forced marriages. Where literature is concerned it is necessary for every reader—whatever his professional or other preoccupations—to meet the play or poem on its own terms, as the curious complicated sort of thing it is, speaking with its own voice (which may be a blend of many voices), and governed by its own conventions of communication. As Harding says of one of Blake's more difficult poems, "repeated listening, with strict moderation in the use of intellectual ingenuities," is the likeliest way of getting at the pressures that shaped the words. There is indeed no substitute for attentive and repeated listening, without an overeagerness to "explain" in terms of some scheme not necessarily intrinsic to the poem. But when we have really listened in this way something may emerge that can be assimilated within a different field of interest by a psychiatrist, a teacher or administrator, or even a politician.

I want to suggest the kind of thing that is going on in *The Winter's Tale*. I shall use some ideas that I have got from reading outside the field of literary studies. But I don't want to pretend to knowledge that I do not possess; and I shall probably be most useful if I speak of the play simply and directly, leaving others to decide how, if at all, the play (and what I say about the play) engages with other interests, such as an interest in psychoanalysis.

Shakespeare's last plays (which he may not have known were his last) in some ways form a group different from the tragedies that preceded them not only because they have happy endings. They are sometimes misleadingly known as romances—misleadingly because the term doesn't do justice to their firm connection with the actual: a connection that we see both in the language—which is firm, pithy, and incisive as well as complex and subtle—and in the nature of the interests aroused: the magic island of *The Tempest*, for example, is a microcosm of the world, and the play is about colonization and politics as well as about the attempts of an aging man to reach some kind of peace with himself. Neither are these plays a homogeneous group: *Pericles* and *Cymbeline* are experiments, and *The Winter's Tale* and *The Tempest* are different from these two plays and from each other.

All the same the last plays do share certain common features. Serious issues are raised—the nature and consequences of human sin and frailty—but all end "happily." Relationships are shattered and renewed. Lost children are found again, and attention is directed not to the "generation gap" (as in *King Lear*) but to the positive effect of young people in bringing some renewal of life to the world of the middle-aged or old. Instead of following through the potentially disastrous consequences of wrong choice, perverted energy, or the clash of rival value-systems, reversal from disaster is brought about through developed insight, repentance, forgiveness, and reconciliation. "Pardon's the word for all": the words of the king in *Cymbeline* cannot be applied with any easy complacency, but they suggest the direction in which these plays are moving.

All these themes are presented in a special way. It is not merely that plot and action violate probability, that magic plays a part (oracles warn and exhort), and that there are improbably successful disguisings and impossible adventures. Most of these features could be paralleled in earlier plays, and if we want to grasp the distinguishing features of the technique of the last plays we need to glance at Shakespeare's whole career. We may put it like this. In the earliest plays you are asked to *observe* a world. It isn't a world of course: it is a play world. But the point is that you are asked to observe. You are interested, you feel sympathy and antipathy, you almost necessarily make judgments—and to that extent you are involved. But in the main you are an onlooker. You may feel, "There, but for the grace of God, go I"; but you don't feel that the play is directly evoking your own potentialities, your own conflicts, and all that life of the emotions which can be handled only through myth, symbol, or poetry. As the plays succeed one another we not only feel that more of our world—the world of shared human experience—is involved in the action, but we sense that the kind of thing the action does tends to become different. It is used to project an inner truth in which each one of us finds some aspect or potentiality of himself. To be sure, when Yeats said that in great tragic drama "it is always ourselves that we see upon the stage," he did not mean that we identify ourselves with the hero, or that we discard our interest in forms of experience other than our own and look for some idealized—or at all events beglamored—ego-image on the stage: any true work of art demands some going out of ourselves, some stretching of the selves that we are, or think we are. Nevertheless the increasing inwardness of Shakespearean drama means that the action as a whole is more designed to embody and make comprehensible universal forms of inner experience, or potential experience, than it is to reflect or correspond to experience in its outward forms. This is a simplification; and the plays themselves don't make a neat pattern of development. For example *Coriolanus* is concerned with the public and observable world, even though it traces public attitudes and actions to their sources in the personal life: it is not in any sense a myth or parable of the inner life. But *King Lear*, in a sense, is; and it is *King Lear*, more than any other of the great tragedies, that looks forward to the final plays. In these, it seems to me, there is a sense in which it is true to say that certain characters and events are part of the experience of a central character, and therefore stand for—or evoke—aspects of the spectator's own personality as he is absorbed in the play. In *Cymbeline* certain sides of the hero, Posthumus, are reflected in the black Iachimo and in "that irregulous devil" Cloten; and all three reflect something in ourselves. Not that this is entirely new in Shakespearean drama. In one sense Iago is an unrecognized part of Othello; and in *King Lear* it is not only the daughters who represent different aspects, or possible aspects, of Lear's own character. It is simply that in the later plays this feature of Shakespeare's drama becomes more insistent. One way of putting it might be to say that the plays move closer to the dream, in which the dreamer is *all* the characters; but I don't want to suggest that the plays are in any way "dreamy" or mere wishful fantasy. In *English Dramatic Form* M. C. Bradbrook speaks of the way in which a play can affect the "internal society" of each individual spectator:

> Participation may correspond to the therapeutic function of a dream, and the final result will not by any means be just a fantasy gratification. The play dynamically frees and flexes relatively fixed and rigid images of the inner society. Therefore, if several roles attract identification, the plot becomes an exercise in the dynamics of adjustment, uniquely assisted by the fact that participation in drama is itself a social act. Conflicts can be projected more directly and more intensively.

Miss Bradbrook is speaking of drama generally, but I think her words are especially apt in relation to Shakespeare's last plays. In these Shakespeare is exploring possible alternatives to disruption and tragedy; he is trying to define the life-enhancing energy that paradoxically was released by the great tragedies, but defining it now not as something glimpsed in and through defeat, but as something that *could* be actualized in daily living. He is especially concerned with what, borrowing the term from psychiatry, we may perhaps call integration, considered both as something taking place within the individual and as a function of relationship between persons.

If you knew *The Winter's Tale* only from an outline of the plot you would conclude that it is a very silly play. The same of course could be said of other great plays in which unlikely stories frame significant human actions. But Shakespeare did more than infuse human interest into a plot adopted from Greene's *Pandosto*. We should see *The Winter's Tale* not primarily as a dramatic action, following the fortunes of certain people, but instead as a poetic and dramatic representation of two contrasting "states" of the human soul and an exploration of the possibility of "metamorphosis" of one state into the other. It seems significant that one of Shakespeare's favorite books, the *Metamorphoses* of Ovid, was much in his mind at this time.

We can best get the sense of what the play is doing if—instead of bothering about probability or even much about characterization—we put side by side two passages in which the poetry is most powerful. They form a contrast on which the whole play turns—and I don't mean contrasts of character; I mean contrasting mental states.

> Thou want'st a rough pash, and the shoots that I have
> To be full, like me: yet they say we are
> Almost as like as eggs; women say so,
> (That will say anything.) But were they false
> As o'er-dyed blacks, as wind, as waters; false
> As dice are to be wish'd, by one that fixes
> No bourn 'twixt his and mine; yet were it true,
> To say this boy were like me. Come (Sir Page)
> Look on me with your welkin eye: sweet villain,
> Most dear'st, my collop: Can thy dam, may't be
> Affection? thy intention stabs the centre.
> Thou dost make possible things not so held,
> Communicat'st with Dreams (how can this be?)
> With what's unreal: thou coactive art,
> And fellow'st nothing. Then 'tis very credent,
> Thou may'st co-join with something, and thou dost,
> (And that beyond commission) and I find it,
> (And that to the infection of my brains,
> And hard'ning of my brows.)

The folio punctuation which I have used for this passage is not unalterable, but I assume that it comes close to Shakespeare's intentions. It is, in any event, impossible to "straighten out" the speech and make it conform to ordinary syntactical forms: the point is its disjointedness. The marked caesuras and the frequent parentheses produce a panting, heaving movement which tells you what to think of the appearance of argument with which Leontes tries to establish his belief. The "thinking" is entirely guided by passion. This speech has been described (by Mark Van Doren in his *Shakespeare*) as "the obscurest passage in Shakespeare," but the general drift is clear. Whatever the precise meaning is of "affection" or "intention," Leontes is trying to establish the validity of an emotional bias by claiming how very reasonable it is to accept it. After all, he says, a strong feeling that a thing is so can sometimes be more valid than common sense ("dost make possible things not so held"), and our intuitions can find truth in dreams. Dreams are "unreal," are "nothings," so if affection can work on such unsubstantial material, how much more likely that it can join with what is actually there. In his concluding lines his mind fairly pounces on his "proof": "Then 'tis very credent, / Thou may'st co-join with something, *and thou dost.*"

It is completely illogical, of course; for it is the existence of the "something" that needs to be proved. But it has a kind of spurious or neurotic logic; and this drive of Leontes' mind is strengthened by the images of great physical intensity, here and elsewhere, through which it is expressed. I do not think we need bother ourselves with the question of the causes of Leontes' disease. I can find no support in the play for J. I. M. Stewart's suggestion that Leontes is projecting on to Hermione his own repressed homosexual feelings for Polixenes. It seems more likely that his jealousy is rooted in a revulsion against his own sexuality and therefore against sexuality in general. But Leontes here is a type of irrational self-justifying suspiciousness that in real life could have many causes. What Shakespeare defines with great clarity in Leontes is, so to speak, a type case of disordered passions. In "The Grammar of Jealousy" J. P. Thorne has shown by a detailed linguistic analysis of Leontes' "insane" speeches how ambiguity, broken syntax, and a kind of fissure in the deep structure of the sentences are used to express a distortion and *parti pris* in the preverbal levels of his thinking.

I shall return to this speech; but now consider the passage I have selected for contrast, again retaining the folio punctuation.

> What you do,
> Still betters what is done. When you speak (Sweet)
> I'ld have you do it ever: when you sing,
> I'ld have you buy, and sell so: so give alms,
> Pray so: and for the ord'ring your affairs,
> To sing them too. When you do dance, I wish you
> A wave o' the sea, that you might ever do
> Nothing but that: move still, still so:

> And own no other function. Each your doing,
> (So singular in each particular)
> Crowns what you are doing, in the present deeds,
> That all your acts, are queens.

The rhythm is obviously very different from that of Leontes' disordered speech. Leontes had said, "My heart dances, But not for joy—not joy." Here the movement and the patterning suggest a dance, even before the word is mentioned. There is a basic order given by the repetitions of the structure ("When you speak, Sweet," "when you sing," "When you do dance") and by the repetition of words ("do" and "doing"—the barest and simplest indication of activity—and "so" and "still"). But there is no monotony: as in a dance there are repetition and variety, order and vitality. The actions that are the objects of this loving attention are all of the simplest and commonest kinds—speaking, singing, buying and selling, giving alms, saying prayers, ordering household affairs; but the "common" is invested with grace and power and appears in all its irreplaceable uniqueness in the present moment.

> When you do dance, I wish you
> A wave o' the sea, that you might ever do
> Nothing but that: move still, still so:
> And own no other function.

Here not only does the line-movement suggest the movement of the wave ("move still, still so"), but the image brings with it further suggestions: just as the breaking of the wave on the shore has behind it the force of the deeper movements of the ocean, so the grace of the dancer is associated with deep "impersonal" forces. In short what the poetry gives you is an image of natural energy, patterned and ordered into expressive forms. And Perdita, we notice, is described—or evoked—in poetry that implies a widening circle of relationship. Leontes' speech is disjointed, broken, passion-ridden; and it comes to a climax on "I" ("and I find it"). It spins on itself with an insane frenzy. Florizel is entirely absorbed in contemplation of the loved person.

These two speeches, then, are polar opposites, representing radically contrasting possibilities of experience, and, put in conjunction, they indicate the inner movement that determines the play's dramatic structure. It is always dangerous to talk about "what

Shakespeare intended"; but you can say that the play seems to ask, and to attempt an answer to, the question: How, if at all, is it possible for the man who utters the first speech to recognize the health of, and so reach out toward, what is represented in the second? What is the possibility of radical metamorphosis?

Acts 1 to 3—the long first movement—are mainly given to creating a sense of Leontes' unbalanced self-enclosure. Poetry and action go together. Throughout the greater part of this movement nothing is in relation. Things are broken off abruptly and without ceremony, like Polixenes' visit and the tale Mamillius begins to tell his mother, which gets no further than "there was a man dwelt by the churchyard." They are seen in sharp contrast, as the domestic quiet of the opening of act 2 is destroyed by the eruption of Leontes' mad fury. There are denial and rejection, as Hermione is repudiated by Leontes, the baby Perdita cast out, and the message of the oracle at first denounced as false. There is a special significance in the contrast, so often insisted on, between infancy and youth on the one hand and adult life on the other. A striking example is when the newly born babe is laid at the feet of the madly jealous Leontes (2.3). Paulina describes it in some detail, so that for a few moments it is vividly there to our imaginations—a physical presence, genuine new life and, Paulina insists, in a clear relationship to the father. But Leontes denies it; he will have the child cast away—in a sense, therefore, denying his own age of innocence.

There is much more in these first three acts that deserves attention—especially the bewildered expostulations of the courtiers as they try to make contact with Leontes' mind; the strangely serene and moving poetry in which Apollo's island of Delos is described (the oracle, says John Vyvyan in *The Shakespearean Ethic*, is "a message to the passions from the spirit"); and Hermione's dignified speech at her trial, where she shows a legitimate concern for her honor, but is less concerned for herself than for her husband. All of this not only acts as a contrast to, and therefore defines, Leontes' paranoiac suspiciousness but will play a part in the total pattern of the play. Above all there is the last scene of act 3, in which, in a setting of storm and disaster, the castaway baby is found by the old shepherd: "Thou met'st with things dying," he says to his son, "I with things new-born." But I must go on to speak, briefly and inadequately, of the great pastoral scene that, after a gap of sixteen years, forms the greater part of act 4.

It isn't easy to say what one wants to about the sheep-shearing scene, because there are no critical terms immediately available. Clearly you can't use psychological terms appropriate to the analysis of character; and at the same time you have to avoid any suggestion of mere allegory. It is a unique achievement, and I don't know anything quite like it, even in Shakespeare. Act 4, scene 4, is devoted to presenting nothing less than a whole, complex but unified, attitude to life. It does this by building up a pattern of relationships, not in any abstract way, but through the movement of our minds and feelings and imagination as we respond to what is concretely given in the dramatic action and the poetry. It is by attending to that pattern, responding to it as fully as we can, that we become aware of new possibilities of living that form the direct antithesis of what has been presented in Leontes. The characteristics of his state of mind, we saw, were self-enclosure, chaos, and the projection of his fantasies. What is given in the evocation of Perdita is a grace of human living, felt intensely in an individual presence, but *related* both to a wider human context and to impersonal forces of generation and growth. The whole of the scene is devoted to giving body to that relationship—not only in the idiom and reference, which range from the homely to the highly imaginative, from the rural and local to the classical and mythological. And all is pervaded by a full and intimate sense of "great creating Nature." Our sense of Perdita comes in the first place from the poetry that she speaks or that is spoken to her. There is no doubt about the grace that lives in her, but she is not in any way cut off from the life that surrounds her. Her speech can be as homely and direct as that of Autolycus and the rustics. Again and again she refers to the everyday things and processes of rural life—the gardener's "dibble," grafting, planting slips, starved sheep in winter, "Whitsun pastorale." It is this that links her to the rustic earthiness of the shepherds, though she goes beyond it. There is nothing of the prude or the flirt in the expression of her love for Florizel.

Perdita and Florizel only exist in the living context that Shakespeare has provided for them. From the opening exchange of the lovers there is a sense of the relation of man, nature, and the "gods." We are constantly but unobtrusively reminded of the daily and seasonal cycle. In late summer Perdita evokes the flowers of the spring.

> O Proserpina,
> For the flowers now that, frighted, thou let'st fall
> From Dis's waggon! daffodils,
> That come before the swallow dares, and take
> The winds of March with beauty; violets, dim,
> But sweeter than the lids of Juno's eyes
> Or Cytherea's breath.

Classical myth—and it is especially appropriate that Proserpine should be invoked—is re-created in terms of the English country-side; and with only a little exaggeration we may say that the whole of an English spring is caught in the two lines about the daffodils—which are tough and resilient ("take / The winds of March") as well as beautiful. It is immediately after this that we have Florizel's lines, "What you do, / Still betters what is done," of which I have already spoken. But a moment later we are back to jokes about garlic ("to mend your kissing with"), "homely foolery," with ballads, rounds, and a dance of twelve satyrs.

It would be easy to see the central contrast embedded in the play as one between neurosis bred by or within civilization and a purely natural spontaneity and directness of living. But the matter is more complicated than that. If we don't take the full force of all that is suggested by Autolycus's song, "The red blood reigns in the Winter's pale"—which, so to speak, carries over into the love-making that follows—we certainly don't possess the play. But equally we don't possess it if we see *only* that. I don't know the current status of the will in psychoanalytical thinking. Certainly a patient can't dissolve a neurosis by will alone: the spurred horse always shies at the same fence. But equally you can't talk about health in any meaningful way without invoking the conception of intent. Lionel Trilling in "Freud and Literature" says:

> What may be called the essentially Freudian view assumes that the mind, for good as well as bad, helps create its reality by selection and evaluation. . . . The reality to which Freud wishes to reconcile the neurotic patient is, after all, a "taken" and not a "given" reality. It is the reality of social life and of value, conceived and maintained by the human mind and will. Love, morality, honour, esteem—these are the components of a created reality.

Such considerations seem relevant here. When, toward the end of this scene, Polixenes, in terms that suggest something like elderly jealousy of the young, forbids the marriage, the poetry moves to the celebration of faithfulness—a quality that is not merely natural but human:

> Not for Bohemia, nor the pomp that may
> Be thereat gleaned; for all the sun sees, or
> The close earth wombs, or the profound seas hide
> In unknown fathoms, will I break my oath
> To this my fair beloved.

It is only with this, the assertion of a love that, very credibly, is not Time's fool, that we can pass to the final image of integration in the last act.

What is meant by integration here is something that can be defined only in terms of a close study of the action and the poetry. We are not dealing with the working out of a plot in terms of a sequence of cause and effect. We are dealing with two contrasting states of the human soul; and when we ask how the one can be changed into the other we find our answer not in the descriptive and analytic terms of psychology, but in terms of a poetry and symbolism that evoke, without fully rationalizing, the deeper movements of mind and feeling. The play's second movement has given us a state of being that offered the strongest possible contrast to the state displayed by Leontes in the opening acts—a spring and summer opposed to Leontes' winter. When the lost daughter returns, she brings with her all the richness of positive living that has been so strongly associated with her. She represents an order of experience that is now, I was tempted to say, available to Leontes. That would be a wrong way of putting it. Instead it is an order of experience within which Leontes can be included. For the image of integration of which I spoke, although it can find a reflection in the mind of each individual beholder, is something that goes beyond the separate characters of the drama. It is composed, enacted, by the whole dramatic pattern, and—contrary to Leontes' jealousy—it is established in a widening circle of relationships.

At the opening of act 5 Leontes' penitence belongs to the same order of experience as Florizel's and Perdita's affirmation of faithfulness and Hermione's legitimate concern for her honor: it is a recognition of absolute human values. It is only with the full and continued recognition of what he has done—resolutely assisted by Paulina—that we hear at his court the note of new life with the entry of the young lovers, who are "welcome hither, / As is the spring to the earth." Florizel, asking for help, links the past and present:

> Beseech you, sir,
> Remember since you owed no more to time
> Than I do now,

—which recalls both "grace and remembrance be to you both" and the nostalgic memories of boyhood that, early in the play, contrasted so markedly with Leontes' adult folly. But the youthful past is no longer felt as simple contrast, and there is no need either to regret or to disown it. I think it is true to say that in these later scenes you have a poetic enactment of Erik Erikson's account in *Insight and Responsibility* of the mutual support and creative interplay that exist between the generations. Jung says in *On the Nature of the Psyche* that the maturing personality "must assimilate the parental complex," a statement that needs to be complemented by one that, as it were, goes in the other direction. The maturing personality must somehow, in Coleridge's words (in *The Friend*), "carry on the feelings of childhood into the powers of manhood." "To find no contradiction in the union of old and new, to contemplate the Ancient of Days with feelings as fresh, as if they then sprang forth at his own fiat, this characterises the minds that feel the riddle of the world, and may help to unravel it." (Blake's poem "The Echoing Green" is a beautiful image of the kind of experience I have been pointing to.) It is not for nothing that, a little later, the old shepherd is described as standing by "like a weather-beaten conduit of many kings' reigns"; the simile suggests a succession of generations that, in the forms of culture, stretches far beyond the span of father and mother and child.

The second scene of the last act consists of the relation of the discovery of Perdita's birth, in which Shakespeare forestalls the objections of literalist critics:

> such a deal of wonder is broken out within this hour, that ballad-makers cannot be able to express it.

> they looked as they had heard of a world ransomed, or one destroyed.

> Every wink of an eye some new grace will be born.

Some of the phrases have religious associations, but the scene as a whole has a down-to-earth quality that relates the profound and the commonplace. On the sea-voyage Perdita had been "much sea-sick," and Florizel "little better." And at the end of the scene we have the naïve pride of the shepherd and his son, a pride that is tempered by the shepherd's natural good breeding, "for we must be gentle, now we are gentlemen." When the shepherd's son expounds the relationships between himself, his father, and their new royal "kindred," the effect is comic but not merely comic: for when, in the clown's words, "the prince my brother and the princess my sister called my father father," we have an echo of Perdita's

> I was not much afeard; for once or twice
> I was about to speak and tell him plainly,
> The selfsame sun that shines upon his court
> Hides not his visage from our cottage, but
> Looks on alike.

As for the final scene, obviously it is possible to see it as a conventional happy ending with a few striking lines of poetry interspersed. But, again, we need to see it in relation to the whole dramatic pattern. Instead of the racy prose of the preceding scene we have poetry with a solemn, ceremonious quality: a rite is being performed. The tempo of the previous scene was one of mounting excitement: here there is a hushed stillness as all eyes center on the supposed statue and the final transformation of the play is enacted. The statue, the wife who for a time had ceased in Leontes' eyes to be the person she was (significantly she is far more wrinkled than when he saw her last), steps down. Within the conventions of the play this is a symbol of that renewal of life which is the main theme of *The Winter's Tale*. The characters, restored to each other in a new naturalness of affection, are restored to life lived in the present, free from the usual mechanisms of distortion. Paulina's words, to the accompaniment of music, are:

> Come!
> I'll fill your grave up: stir, nay, come away:
> Bequeath to death your numbness; for from him
> Dear life redeems you.

There is an echo here of Autolycus's song about the daffodils and the red blood. He is not present at the final revelation; but he is, very properly, in Sicily, and not far off.

After the winter of sin and separation, however, it is not merely "red blood" or natural impulse that reigns: it is natural impulse purified by something for which Shakespeare uses the religious word *grace*. Northrop Frye says (in *Fables of Identity*) that "such grace is not Christian or theological grace, which is superior to the order of nature, but a secular analogy of Christian grace which is identical with nature." I am sure Frye is right to make the distinction between grace as used in *The Winter's Tale* and theological grace. But grace in the play's sense isn't really "identical with nature." There is no divorce and absolute discontinuity between them. Grace, here, is a consummation of that naturalness and spontaneity that were so beautifully evoked in the pastoral scene. It can only enter when nature has been, not disowned, but enlisted in the cause of "honesty" and "honour," love and trust—human values and commitments of which nature by itself knows nothing.

With the paradoxical combination of intimacy and distancing characteristic of great dramatic art, *The Winter's Tale* works in two different ways to one end. Insofar as the different characters represent different possibilities of experience for the individual self, it explores some of the ways of growing into wholeness, which involves not only the—sometimes painful—withdrawal of projections, but also a continuing openness to different kinds of life. Although the play as a whole is received by different individual minds (just as it was created by one mind), it is received *as if* it enacted relations between persons inhabiting a common world; and to grasp it in the second of these aspects is, curiously, the best way of understanding it as a *psychomachia* or internal "conflict of the soul." And in this way, as in others, art "imitates" life. In *Organic Unity in Coleridge* Gordon McKenzie comments on Coleridge's idea of individuation in his essay "Theory of Life":

> To the common-sense view, individuality frequently means that which is unique or peculiar to one person; its essence lies in something strong in itself and sharply detached from life around it. Individualism or individuality is often directly opposed to universality or catholicity. This is not true of Coleridge, who looks upon individuality as some-

thing strong in itself, to be sure, but more particularly as a force which reaches out and makes new connections and relations. The greatest individuality is that which has the greatest degree of organization, the largest quantity of relations.

That, however, is merely statement, admirably as it is made. Shakespeare's play, by calling out the energies of the mind, makes us—in ways that are not fully open to introspection—*live through* movements of mind, feeling, sympathy, that have to be experienced as parts of ourselves. No more than *The Tempest* does *The Winter's Tale* offer a "solution" that can be applied. It is simply that in responding, trying to understand, the mind *grows toward* the experience of which the play is a living image: it moves toward an idea of wholeness that can nourish our living, even when we are—as is usually the case—not whole.

Women and Issue in *The Winter's Tale*

Carol Thomas Neely

Most critics have seen the final reconciliations in *The Winter's Tale* as the triumph of time, of the gods, of nature, or of art. These large extrapersonal forces inform every aspect of the play. But they work their miracles only through the play's characters, particularly its women. Hermione, Paulina, and Perdita are in league with time, nature, and the play's pagan gods by virtue of their acceptance of "issue" and of all that this central idea implies—sexuality and childbirth, separation and change, growth and decay. By their presence and their actions they teach men to accept life's rhythms. C. L. Barber has said that in the romantic comedies,

> the perverse and repressive are laughed out of court while release leads to the embrace of passion, sanctioned by clarification as to its place as part of the natural cycle. In the romances, however, fulfilment for the principal figure requires a transformation of love, not simply liberation of it.

In the romantic comedies women were the catalysts to love's "liberation"; in *The Winter's Tale* they are the workers of its "transformation." Here, for the first time since those comedies, women use wit and realism in the service of passion to mock male folly, to educate men, and to achieve a fruitful union with them.

Rosalind, Viola, Portia, and the women in *Love's Labour's Lost*

From *Philological Quarterly* 57, no. 2 (Spring 1978). © 1978 by the University of Iowa.

all have active roles in their plays, grounding male idealism in reality and effecting a reconciliation of sex with love, wit with affection, male with female. In the tragedies, however, powerful women—Lady Macbeth, Goneril and Regan, Volumnia, Cleopatra—are destructive, while the women who inherit the virtues of the comedy heroines—Portia, Juliet, Ophelia, Desdemona, Emilia, Cordelia—are powerless and are destroyed. Even the women in the other romances—Thaisa and Marina, Imogen, Miranda—important as they may be as symbolic figures, are on the periphery of the action and are controlled and defined by others. But in *The Winter's Tale* efficacy and fruitfulness are reunited in the women. The play's regenerations and reunions, its "issues," are, in large measure, their triumph.

The Winter's Tale, like *Othello*, whose story it will transform, begins in a limited masculine world which, lacking an Iago, appears to be entirely harmonious and self-sufficient. It purports to control time and space through the ideal changeless friendship of Leontes and Polixenes and through the ideal prince Mamillius, who "makes old hearts fresh" and will perpetuate Leontes' kingdom. Women are strikingly absent from the idyllic picture drawn by Camillo and Archidamus. They are the "matter" (1.1.35) which threatens it but will become the source of a harmony richer and less fragile than this one. Though the play begins without mention of women, it concludes with an extended acknowledgment of their power and centrality: the breathtaking rejuvenation of Hermione and of her marriage is followed by the climactic reunion of Hermione and Perdita, the granting of a husband to Paulina as reward for her exploits (a startling reversal of the conventions of old tales), and the reestablishment—at the last—of the friendship of Hermione and Polixenes. I will examine the ways in which the women in the play function to achieve and deserve this conclusion, preserving themselves and educating men to "see the issue" (5.3.128).

Leontes' jealousy in the opening acts is a darker, more dangerous version of the foolishness of the comedy heroes. His "weakhinged fancy" (2.3.117) creates the objects of jealousy as the comedy lovers created the objects of their love; he, like Theseus, recognizes the mechanics of this process; "With what's unreal thou coactive art, / And fellow'st nothing" (1.2.141–42). As the lovers conventionalized the objects of their love into ideal Petrarchan mistresses, so in his jealousy Leontes transforms Hermione into an abstract "hobby-horse," (1.2.276) a "thing" (2.1.82). He adopts the conventional gestures and responses of the cuckold with as much relish as the lovers adopted their roles: "Go play, boy, play: thy mother plays, and I / Play too—but so disgraced a part, whose issue / Will hiss me to my grave" (1.2.187–89). He creates extravagantly out of nothing the promiscuity of the adulterers and the gossip of the court. Then, in the fashion of Othello, he allegorizes his predicament into a comfortingly commonplace drama ("Should all despair, / That have revolted wives, the tenth of mankind / Would hang themselves" (1.2.198–200).

At the root of Leontes' folly are his divorce of sexuality from love and his resulting vacillation—resembling Othello's—between the idealization and degradation of women. Both Leontes and Polixenes are nostalgic for their innocent pre-sexual boyhood when each had a "dagger muzzled, / Lest it should bite its master" (1.2.156–57), and their "weak spirits" were not yet "higher reared / With stronger blood" (1.2.72–73). Both blame their "fall" into sexuality on women, who are "devils" (1.2.82), seductive and corrupting. The boyhood friendship, continued unchanged across time and space, is a protection against women, sex, change, and difference. It is no wonder Leontes wants Polixenes to stay longer in Sicily!

If the kings' friendship with each other takes precedence over their relationship with their wives, so too does their intimacy with their sons. But this relationship is corrupted as well. Their affection for their sons is as narcissistic and stifling as their affection for each other. The fathers see their children as copies of themselves, extensions of their own egos, guarantees of their own innocence. Just as Polixenes describes the friends as "twinned lambs" (1.2.67), so Leontes repeatedly insists that his son is "like me" (1.2.129). Polixenes' description, in which Leontes concurs, of the self-justifying use he makes of his son sums up the attitudes of both toward their children:

> He's all my exercise, my mirth, my matter;
> Now my sworn friend, and then mine enemy;
> My parasite, my soldier, statesman, all.
> He makes a July's day short as December,
> And with his varying childness, cures in me
> Thoughts that would thick my blood.
>
> (1.2.166–71)

But the children do not "cure" their fathers; instead, the men's corrupted views of sexuality are projected onto their children. Mamillius, since not created by some variety of male parthenogenesis as Leontes would seem to prefer, is declared infected by his physical connection with Hermione:

> I am glad you did not nurse him;
> Though he does bear some signs of me, yet you
> Have too much blood in him.
>
> (2.1.56–58)

Eventually he sickens and dies from the strength of Leontes' repudiation of the physical integrity of his mother and himself. Later in Bohemia, Polixenes—extraordinarily—views his son's rebelliousness as comparable to Leontes' loss: "Kings are no less unhappy, their issue not being gracious, than they are in losing them when they have approved their virtues" (4.2.28–30). His tirade just before he reveals himself suggests that he views his son's achievement of sexual maturity as confirmation of his own impotence, as deterioration into second, unwelcome childhood. ("Is not your father grown incapable / Of reasonable affairs? Is he not stupid / With age and alt'ring rheums? . . . Lies he not bed-rid? And again does nothing / But what he did being childish?" [4.4.401–5].) His vicious suggestive attack on Perdita (whom up to this point he had admired) reveals nakedly the distaste for women wittily apparent in his tales of boyhood and pompously implicit in his discussion of grafting to "make conceive a bark of baser kind / By bud of nobler race" (4.4.94–95). She, like Hermione before her, is seen as a whore, "the angle that plucks our son thither" (4.2.49). Polixenes now worries about the infection of his blood and threatens to eliminate Florizel from it as Leontes has already eliminated Hermione, Perdita, and, indirectly, Mamillius. Ironically, by denying their children freedom, difference, and sexual maturity, the two men deny themselves with continuity, potency, and regeneration they need and desire but which cannot be achieved by their own return, through their children, to a false ideal of childhood innocence.

Just as the romantic comedies are rich with reminders of the physical realities which the heroes neglect—"If a cat will after kind, / So be sure will Rosalind. / Wintred garments must be lined, / So must slender Rosalind" (3.2.102–5)—so too is *The Winter's Tale*. Imagery of breeding, and, especially, of birth pervades the play at all levels, countering the courtiers' tendency toward refinement and abstraction. Submerged metaphorical references are everywhere ("What may chance / Or breed upon our absence" (1.2.11–12); "Temptations have since then been born to 's" (1.2.77). Hermione's pregnancy and delivery receive much literal attention. Birth is proscribed in Antigonus's threat to geld his daughters so they won't "bring false generations" (2.1.148) and is parodied when the Shepherd and Clown become "gentlemen born" in the last act. The notion of birth underlies almost all of the play's major speeches and scenes: Leontes' "Affection! Thy intention stabs the center" speech (1.2.138–46); the messengers' return from Delphos when they pray, "Gracious be the issue" (3.1.22); the old shepherd's central line, "Thou met'st with things dying, / I with things new born" (3.3.112–13); Time's description of his role as the ultimate father-creator; Polixenes' grafting scheme for the purpose of conceiving new stock; the narrated reunion where, in spite of the "broken delivery," "truth" is made "pregnant" by "circumstance" (5.2.10, 33–34); where, "every wink of an eye, some new grace will be born" (5.2.118–19); and the reanimation of the statue which imitates the gradual process of birth. As the play proceeds the literal birth of Perdita is reiterated and transformed in a series of rebirths, but these retain emotional and symbolic ties with the process which Paulina most explicitly and eloquently describes:

> The child was prisoner to the womb and is
> By law and process of great Nature thence
> Freed, and enfranchised.
>
> (2.2.59–61)

The women in the play, participating in and accepting this process, are the "cure" for the "thoughts" that "thick" Leontes' and Polixenes' "blood." They are witty where the men are solemn, they are at ease with sex where the men are uneasy about it, and they take for granted change and separation. While mocking male folly, they provide an initiation into the realities of love, sex, marriage, and children. In them we have Shakespeare's final marvelous transformations of the roles of good wife, shrew, and beloved.

Hermione's character and role have been much praised but little analyzed by critics. The extraordinary dignity and control with which she responds to Leontes' accusations have obscured her earlier vivacity. In the opening scene she is remarkable for her wit, her sexual frankness, and her overt affection for Leontes. She takes pleasure in competing verbally with men—"A lady's 'Verily' is / As potent as a lord's" (1.2.50–51), she remarks to Polixenes (and the play will more than bear this out). But, though quick and sharp, her wit is inevitably good-natured and affectionate. She uses her persuasion of Polixenes as occasion to emphasize her love for Leontes: "yet, good deed, Leontes, / I love thee not a jar o' th' clock behind / What lady she her lord" (1.2.42–44). And after talking Polixenes into staying, she diplomatically pacifies him by drawing him out on his favorite topic—the boyhood friendship. She wittily denies Polixenes' notion that marital sex implies "offenses" (1.2.82) and goes on to counsel Leontes in the appropriate management of it: "you may ride's / With one soft kiss a thousand furlongs, ere / With spur we heat an acre" (1.2.94–96).

Her relationship to her children is similarly healthy, free, physical. She affirms her physical ties to them: Mamillius is "the first fruits of my body" (3.2.95), and Perdita, her babe, is "from my breast, / The innocent milk in its most innocent mouth / Haled out to murder" (3.2.97–99). But she does not use her children to reflect herself. At the beginning of act 2, scene 1, in one of the most apt of the play's numerous realistic touches, she is quite simply tired of Mamillius: "he so troubles me, / 'Tis past enduring" (2.1.1–2). Later, when she is "for [him] again," she asks *him* to tell *her* a tale rather than imposing tales on him as Leontes does. Leontes, reinterpreting Hermione's "actions," "dreams" a horror story (3.2.80), and her power to reach him is lost. His fantasy dominates the first three acts. With his denial of her particularity, her words, her sexuality, her offspring, she dies to him.

But Hermione remains a powerful presence in the play. Indeed, she must be seen as its very human deity. Northrop Frye defines the dream visions of Diana in *Pericles* and Jupiter in *Cymbeline* as "an emblematic recognition scene, in which we are shown the power that brings about the comic resolution" and in which "the controlling deity appears with an announcement of what is to conclude the action." Similarly, Hermione appears to Antigonus in a dream vision in which she is transformed into an emblematic figure, "In pure white robes, / Like very sanctity" (3.3.21–22). Alive, she was not "prone to weeping" (2.1.108), but in the vision, "her eyes / Became two spouts"; alive, she was never at a loss for words, but here she is "gasping to begin some speech"

(3.3.24–25). She instructs Antigonus as Diana instructs Pericles, and she narrates the conclusion of the first part of the play as Jupiter does the conclusion of *Cymbeline*. Although Antigonus interprets the vision to mean that Hermione is guilty and dead, it is emblematic rather of the vitality of her fierce love and grief for her daughter; this love informs the remainder of the play.

As deity, she resembles most closely the goddess of fertility, Ceres, with whom she is linked by Perdita's association of herself in act 4 with Ceres' daughter, Persephone. Critics have noted the relevance of the myth's cyclical motif to the play but have paid little attention to the narrative parallels between the two works. Ovid's tale focuses on Ceres' grief at her daughter's loss and on her frantic efforts to be reunited with Persephone. Unable to find her, Ceres takes vengeance on the land, especially Sicily, where the rape occurred:

> She marrde the seede, and eke forbade the fieldes to
>   yeelde their frute.
> The plenteousnesse of that same Ile of which there went
>   such brute
> Through all the world, lay dead: the corne was killed
>   in the blade:
> Now too much drought, now too much wet did make
>   it for to fade.

Having learned that Persephone was stolen by Pluto and is now queen of the underworld, "Her mother stoode as starke as stone, when she these newes did heare, / And long she was like one that in another worlde had beene" (632–33). (Perhaps this story as well as that of Pygmalion suggested the statue scene to Shakespeare.) Because of the consummation of the rape Persephone cannot be fully re-integrated with her mother but is returned to her for six months of the year. When reunited with her daughter, Ceres rejuvenates the earth, just as when Perdita returns to Sicily, its barren winter ends, its air is purged of "infection" (5.1.169), and spring is at hand. Persephone, Sandys says in his commentary on the story, represents "the fertility of the seed" in the play as in the myth Sicily's "fail of issue" (5.1.27) is the direct result of the absence of Hermione and Perdita.

If Hermione is the presiding deity of the play, Paulina is her priestess whose power lies in her "medicinal words" (2.3.36) as she recognizes and as Leontes eventually acknowledges. But although early in the play Leontes tries to reduce her to the comically unattractive role of shrew, she transforms and transcends the role. She acts not out of ill will but, like Emilia in *Othello*, out of love for her mistress and, like Kate and Beatrice, out of affection for the man she "baits." She believes Leontes is salvageable—and worth saving. So, unlike Camillo, she sticks out the task to its conclusion. Her attacks on Leontes, unlike those of Antigonus, are calculated, judicious, positive. While attacking Leontes' folly, she offers him alternatives to it. She first urges him to accept and bless Perdita, using the argument, designed to please him and to dispel his suspicions, that the child is "the whole matter / And copy of the father" (2.3.97–98). After her tirade against Leontes following Hermione's "death," Paulina offers him one last chance to "see" Hermione—"if you can bring / Tincture or luster in her lip, her eye, / Heat outwardly or breath within, I'll serve you / As I would do the gods" (3.2.202–5). Finally, she presents him with an image of penance which he accepts as the commencement of his "recreation" (1.238).

Paulina, sharing many of Hermione's qualities and present when she is absent, is a surrogate for her mistress. But she can lead Leontes toward a reunion with Hermione as Hermione herself cannot because she assumes an unthreatening, asexual role. We are reminded of the literal disguises which freed Julia, Rosalind, and Viola to communicate with their beloveds. At first, Paulina takes on an explicitly masculine identity. Bringing Perdita to Leontes, she substitutes for the "minister of honor" (2.2.49) Hermione feared to approach. Arriving, she urges the timid lords to "be second" (2.3.26) to her and later makes explicit her warrior's role—"[I] would by combat make her good, so were I / A man, the worst about you" (2.3.59–60). But after Leontes has accepted Hermione's innocence and Paulina's tutelage, Paulina changes her strategy. She makes as if to drop her loquaciousness ("I'll say nothing" [3.2.230]) and identifies herself as a woman subordinate to Leontes—"Now, good my liege, / Sir, royal sir, forgive a foolish woman" (3.2.224–25). She is now no longer the "mankind witch" (2.3.66) of her first scene with Leontes but a "good lady" (3.2.172) who closely resembles Hermione. By act 5, scene 1, Paulina and Leontes have achieved understanding and reciprocity; their long, intimate, chaste friendship is a transformation and vindication of Hermione's and Polixenes'.

As Hermione's virtues are regenerated for Leontes in Paulina, they are regenerated for the audience in Perdita. In her flower speeches with their embrace of change and pity for maidenhood, in her image of Florizel as "a bank for Love to lie and play on" (4.4.130), and in her easy assumption that Florizel should "Desire to breed by me" (4.4.103), Perdita expresses a frank and whole-hearted acceptance of sexuality that recalls Hermione's in the opening scenes. She shares too with her mother and Paulina what Tillyard calls her "ruthless common sense" and employs it as wittily and adeptly as they to deflate men's exaggerated rhetoric and vapid generalizations—whether Camillo's about "affliction" (4.4.579) or Polixenes' about art and nature.

But Perdita is important not only as character and symbol but also for the responses which she generates, for the healthy relationships in which she participates. Florizel, in comparison with the heroes of the comedies, with even a Romeo or an Othello, but especially with a Leontes, is a remarkable lover. His courtship, unlike Leontes' "crabbèd" (1.2.102) one, is joyous and confident. He acknowledges Perdita's sexuality and his own, identifying himself with the gods who have "taken / The shapes of beasts upon them" (4.4.26–27) but controlling his burning "lusts" (1.34). He delights in Perdita's frankness, her beauty, her wit, in her "blood" which look[s] out" (4.4.160). His unconventional praise of her—"When you speak, sweet, / I'd have you do it ever" (4.4.136)—reveals his appreciation of her singularity. He praises not her looks, but her "deeds"—each of them—reversing Leontes' disgust at Hermione's second "good deed" and purifying the word's sexual implications.

As Florizel is a model lover, so the old shepherd is a model father; his relationship with his children is at every point contrasted with Leontes'. Believing, like Leontes, that Perdita is a bastard (although not, of course, his), he takes her up "for pity" (3.3.75). He does not treat his children as possessions but rather as friends whose independence he respects and whose innocence he knows better than to count on. He makes Perdita mistress of the feast and urges her to "lay it on" (4.3.41–42), to behave with the boldness, warmth, and flirtatiousness embodied in his remarkable reminiscence of his dead wife:

> When my old wife lived, upon
> This day, she was both pantler, butler, cook;
> Both dame and servant; welcomed all, served all;

> Would sing her song, and dance her turn; now here
> At upper end o' th' table, now i' th' middle;
> On his shoulder, and his; her face o' fire
> With labor and the thing she took to quench it,
> She would to each one sip.
>
> (4.4.55–62)

The shepherd's praise of his wife resembles Florizel's more formal praise of Perdita—in its rhythms, its repetitions, its emphasis on particular and multiple actions, and its reference to singing and dancing. Appreciating his wife's sexuality, he accepts Perdita's, encourages her romance and betrothal—"I think there is not half a kiss to choose / Who loves another best" (4.4.176).

The shepherd, like all the inhabitants of the Bohemian countryside, views youth as a period of wantonness, not innocence. He contemplates with exasperated tolerance the age "between ten and three-and-twenty" occupied with "getting wenches with child, wronging the ancientry, stealing, fighting" (3.3.58–62). He speaks from experience, it seems, for the clown tells him, "You're a made old man; if the sins of your youth are forgiven you" (3.3.119–20). The "delicate burden" of Autolycus's ballad urges, "Jump her, and, thump her" (4.4.194–96), for chastity is temporary and unnatural in the fourth act of *The Winter's Tale*. Better to be the usurer's wife, "brought to bed of twenty money-bags at a burden" (4.4.264–65) than to be the woman "turned into a cold fish for she would not exchange flesh with one that loved her" (11.281–82). "Red blood reigns" throughout the act as in Autolycus's introductory song; all are caught in its pulsing rhythms, even—temporarily—Camillo and Polixenes, enthusiastic participants who welcome the rough satyrs' dance by the "men of hair" (4.4.330).

Meanwhile, red blood is thawing in Sicily as well. Returning there in act 5, we discover that Leontes has not been simply worn down by a winter of abstinence and penance, "naked, fasting, / Upon a barren mountain" (3.2.209–10)—in effect a bleaker form of the eternal summer of youth which he with Polixenes had longed for, equally changeless, sexless, endless. Instead he has been changed, regenerated. His transformation is apparent in his acknowledgment of guilt, his chastened rhetoric, but most of all in his new apprehension of Hermione. She is seen no longer as a conventional abstraction, but as a unique woman—"no more such wives, therefore no wife" (5.1.56). He now honors her sexuality as "the sweet'st companion that e'er man / Bred his hopes out of" (5.1.11–12), and he longs for her kisses (and for her words as well): "Then, even now, / I might have looked upon my queen's full eyes, / Have taken treasure from her lips" (5.1.52–54). He is also able, with Paulina's help, to conceive of her as human, flawed, "soul-vexed" (1.59)—liable like himself to jealousy, anger, vengefulness, and berating him on his choice of a new wife.

Leontes' recovery of his wife prepares him for a renewed and transformed relationship with Perdita and Florizel and with Polixenes. The sight of the children once again brings back memories of the boyhood friendship—not of innocence, but of "something wildly / By us performed before" (5.1.129–30). He and Polixenes are no longer "twinned lambs" but have "branched now." Throughout the scene Leontes contrasts himself with his friend, and, discovering that Perdita and Florizel have eloped, he breaks with Polixenes to become "friend" to the couple's "desires" (5.1.230–31). Florizel begs him, "Remember since you owed no more to Time / Than I do now; with thought of such affections / Step forth mine advocate" (ll. 217–20); Leontes does exactly this. His reference to Perdita as a "precious mistress" (l. 223) and his too-youthful gazes at her reveal, not incestuous desires as in *Pandosto*, but Leontes' acceptance of his own courtship and his own desire to "enjoy" Hermione: "I thought of her, / Even in these looks I made" (ll. 227–28).

Leontes' willingness to identify his own affections with the couple's precipitates the multiple recognition scene with Camillo, Perdita, and Polixenes. Even this scene is filled with the presence of Hermione; hers and Perdita's longings for each other generate the final scene. Hermione, like the old subjects in the first scene of the play, has not been "content to die," but has "desire[d]" her "life" to "see" Perdita a woman (1.1.42–44). Perdita in turn, although now blessed with three fathers, a brother, lover, and a mother of sorts in Paulina, yearns for contact with her natural mother "that ended when I but began" (5.3.45). Leontes, however, is the most active participant in the final scene, for it is his recovery of Hermione which explains and facilitates the other reunions.

The final scene then is symbolic—among so much else—of Leontes' acceptance of Hermione as fully his wife. As Othello, at the last, transformed the sleeping Desdemona into "monumental alabaster," so Leontes, at the first, would have preferred, in a sense, a Hermione who was a statue. He distrusted her wit, her warmth, her blood ("You charge him too coldly," Hermione complained to him, and his delusion erupted with the words, "Too hot, too hot" [1.2.30, 108]). Now he explicitly longs for her "warm life," her "blood," her "breath," her speech (5.3.35, 65, 79), and he imbues the statue with them. His determination to kiss the statue signals Paulina that he is ready for reunion with the woman, Hermione. But the moment of reunion is as painful, laborious (and exhilarating) as birth. Paulina, acting as midwife for both, must urge Hermione out of numbness and then must stop Leontes from rejecting her once again:

> Do not shun her
> Until you see her die again, for then
> You kill her double. Nay, present your hand.
> When she was young, you wooed her; now, in age,
> Is she become the suitor?
>
> (5.3.105–9)

The original courtship reversed (into one more like those in the comedies), its sourness perhaps alleviated, Leontes accepts Hermione's embrace, registering his concrete, physical delight: "Oh, she's warm! / If this be magic, let it be an art / Lawful as eating" (ll. 109–11). But the reunion with Leontes is not the final, or perhaps even the central one for Hermione, who, after all, had never rejected Leontes. Her own renewal is completed only when she speaks to Perdita, bestowing on her the blessing the daughter asks for, refused by Leontes so long ago:

> You gods look down,
> And from your sacred vials pour your graces
> Upon my daughter's head! Tell me, mine own,
> Where hast thou been preserved? Where lived? How found
> Thy father's court? For thou shalt hear that I,
> Knowing by Paulina that the oracle
> Gave hope thou wast in being, have preserved
> Myself to see the issue.
>
> (5.3.121–28)

Leontes has been preserved and renewed by Paulina. Perdita has been preserved by time and nature and her foster family in the Bohemian countryside. But Hermione, like Paulina, bereft of husband and future, has preserved herself to see both Perdita and "the issue" in a wider sense: the outcome, "Time's news," which is "known when 'tis brought forth" (4.1.26–27). To achieve this joyous alliance with the processes of time, Hermione is willing to wait out the sixteen years, to accept wrinkles, and to risk a reunion with Leontes. Like her, Paulina, although still grieving for her own lost husband, accepts the new one her "worth and honesty" (5.3.144) merits and begins her own new life. Fittingly, she leads the group "hence" as she had led them hither.

This reading of *The Winter's Tale* suggests some respects in which it differs from the other romances. Although family reunions and the rejuvenation of family relationships are at the heart of all of the plays, in none of the others do fully developed women characters play central active roles. Diana has more effect on the action of *Pericles* than does the sketched-in Thaisa. *Cymbeline*'s Queen, effectively malevolent at the start, is nonetheless a pasteboard figure. In *The Tempest* the evil mother is reduced to Sycorax, Caliban's nightmare, while the good mother, Miranda's, is only a vaguely cherished memory. The daughters fare better. But Marina exists largely to be buffeted by fortune and to redeem Pericles; her own development is not explored. Imogen, the most fully developed and complex woman in the romances, acts resolutely at every opportunity, but all her actions, like her grief for the headless Cloten, are rendered curiously futile or grotesque. Like Isabella and Helena in the problem comedies, she is forever placed in situations where her energies are thwarted, her virtues unrealized. Miranda is a token woman in *The Tempest*, the object of Caliban's lust, Ferdinand's love, and Prospero's plot. *Pericles, Cymbeline,* and *The Tempest* are dominated and controlled by men or by divine agencies who step in when the men prove helpless.

The other romances lack too *The Winter's Tale*'s manifestations of healthy sexuality. All of them hover uneasily between the extreme idealization of sex and its extreme degradation. In *Pericles* there is no realized antidote to the incest motif and the brothel apart from Marina's vehement defense of chastity. In *Cymbeline* there are no characters to counter Iachimo's salacious voyeurism, Cloten's crude obscenity, and Posthumus's exaggerated anti-feminism. In that play the pastoral scenes are all retreat: limited, protected, asexual. Their innocent apparently all-male family renders them more like the nostalgic boyhood of Polixenes' memory than like the

Bohemian countryside. In the whole of *The Tempest*, as in the pastoral scenes of *Cymbeline*, sexuality is controlled or sublimated out of existence. Caliban is ruthlessly confined to slavery for his desire to "people the isle with Calibans." Ferdinand and Miranda are incessantly harangued on chastity by Prospero though neither seems likely to succumb to "th' fire i' th' blood" (4.1.53). Sex and fertility make a brief artful appearance only in Prospero's wedding masque. Nowhere in the other romances is there the easy joyous acceptance of sexuality and procreation which, beyond the confines of Leontes' diseased imagination, comes to dominate *The Winter's Tale*. Perhaps it is these differences which make *The Winter's Tale*, alone among the romances, seem without strain or contrivance. Only in it do the final reunions work symbolically *and* dramatically *and* psychologically, for only here are the women who are crucial to them accepted into the play as fully human figures, "freed" and "enfranchised" from imprisoning roles and imprisoning conceptions projected on them by foolish men.

Tragic Structure in *The Winter's Tale:* The Affective Dimension

Charles Frey

To judge by the classifications of plays in the First Folio, Shake-speare's colleagues, if not Shakespeare himself, thought *The Winter's Tale* and *The Tempest* comedies and *Cymbeline* a tragedy. Of *Pericles*, it seems, they scarcely thought at all, for that play was omitted from their collection. Only after two hundred and fifty years of study were the four plays identified as written consecutively and late in Shakespeare's career. When, about a century ago, scholars began to term the plays "romances" and then even to group them, in collected editions, under that separate heading, they opened a brilliant chapter in Shakespearean interpretation. Not only did the generic label "romance" suggest that there were significant correla-tions among the plays—correlations which might set them off from all the rest in the fashion that "problem" plays or "Roman" plays are sometimes set off—but also the focus upon romance suggested the special relevance of a literary tradition invested with awesome age, universality, and power.

Romance, the dominant mode of fiction-making numbering among its heroes Odysseus, Alcestis, Apollonius of Tyre, the knights of Charlemagne and Arthur, protagonists of Spenser, Sidney, Greene, Cervantes, and thousands more, usually tells, of course, the ele-mental story of journey and, sometimes, of return. Return, forgive-ness, and reconciliation are much stressed in Shakespeare's romance, and those who, like Edward Dowden, first applied the term did so

From *Shakespeare's Romances Reconsidered*, edited by Carol McGinnis Kay and Henry E. Jacobs. © 1978 by the University of Nebraska Press.

to suggest the plays' aura of post-tragic acceptance and benign spirituality:

> Characteristics of versification and style, and the enlarged place given to scenic spectacle, indicate that these plays were produced much about the same time. But the ties of deepest kinship between them are spiritual. There is a certain romantic element in each. They receive contributions from every portion of Shakespeare's genius, but all are mellowed, refined, made exquisite; they avoid the extremes of broad humour and of tragic intensity; they were written with less of passionate concentration than the plays which immediately precede them, but with more of a spirit of deep or exquisite recreation.

Today, while we are grateful for the insights of an earlier age into Shakespeare's recreative spirit of romance, we may doubt that he eschewed "tragic intensity" or that he wrote these plays with less than "passionate concentration." We are, indeed, rediscovering for ourselves both the seriousness and craft of romance, and we are finding in the vaults of Shakespeare's late plays both dark chambers to be explored and curious treasures that may defy the light.

One speaks of dark chambers, because in each Shakespearean romance a motive power of plot arises from the mind's fascination with familial taboo. *Pericles* opens upon the theme of incest. Posthumus Leonatus, in *Cymbeline*, and Leontes, in *The Winter's Tale*, both accuse their wives of adultery. Posthumus himself was bred in Cymbeline's bedchamber and yet secretly married Imogen, making himself thus "poison to Cymbeline's blood." Prospero says of his usurping brother: "he was / The ivy which had hid my princely trunk, / And suck'd my verdure out on't" (1.2.85–87). These perceptions of over-close relations in the plays, relations that threaten the place of potency of each hero, may be associated with a loss of power to procreate sons, for in each play the ruler who conceives a daughter is bereft of wife and any sons he may already have. Perhaps a king in a patrilineal society who sires a daughter is deemed guilty of less than ideal potency and hence subject to usurpation. Or perhaps, as *Pericles* suggests, the sad function of a daughter who is an only child, at least in the world of romance, is not to stay at home where her father may find her sexually tempting but instead to travel into strange lands and there win a husband—

preferably, it turns out, the son of her father's chief enemy to whom her father can now be reconciled.

Whether or not we understand its origins, separation of wives and daughters from husbands and home remains a chief feature of Shakespearean romance, and some sort of familial over-closeness, real or imagined, often initiates the action. We need to explore more fully how the romances portray man's mistrust and mistreatment of woman and with what dramatic impact. In *The Winter's Tale*, the jealousy of Leontes and its consequences are made manifest through a passionate concentration of forms that reach, surely, that tragic intensity Dowden denied to the romances.

During the first three acts of *The Winter's Tale*, Leontes appears four times and each time does the same thing: he denounces Hermione or her surrogate, Paulina, and is rebuked by representatives of his court. To be more precise, in a theme with little variation, Leontes four times expresses his misogyny, separates mother from child, and confronts indignant bystanders. Even if the play were dumb show, this reenacted emblem of blighted affection would work deep into the consciousness of spectators.

During his first appearance onstage (1.2), Leontes watches Hermione as she holds Polixenes' hand; they withdraw from him, and soon he dismisses Mamillius. His violent argument with Camillo follows. In the third scene, he comes upon Hermione and Mamillius, pulls the boy from her, forces them to separate exits, and faces the rebukes of Antigonus and the lords. The fifth scene shows the king attacking and dismissing Paulina and banishing Perdita in the arms of her defender, Antigonus. In the seventh scene, the trial scene, Leontes attacks Hermione, loses Mamillius and her, and suffers the stinging rebuke of Paulina.

The purpose of this reduplicating structure is not primarily to advance the plot, nor is it to explore the motivations of the king. It serves instead to amplify the dimensions of his nightmare and to demonstrate in wider ambit the consequences of his condition. An audience will persist in finding Leontes mad, but will find it harder and harder to ignore the implications of that madness. His idiom spawns violence, and the audience sees an increasingly violent series of expulsions:

Bear the boy hence. (2.1.59)

Away with her, to prison! (2.1.103)

> Go, do our bidding; hence! (2.1.125)
>
> Leave me solely; go. (2.3.17)
>
> Away with that audacious lady! (2.3.42)
>
> Hence with her, out o' door! (2.3.68)
>
> Will you not push her out? (2.3.74)

As the audience hears Leontes conceive his jealousy, accuse Hermione, debate Paulina, and conduct the trial, it also sees him rejecting advice, dismissing women, losing company, being left alone, so that, while he orally projects an image of alienated man, he iconographically enacts the part as well.

Many of the exits away from Leontes, moreover, are lingering and pointed. Twenty-five lines elapse between his first command to Mamillius—"Go, play" (1.2.187)—and the completed exit. Nearly as many form the interval between his dismissal of Hermione and her exit, and then the queen delivers a pointed withdrawal speech:

> Who isn't that goes with me? . . .
>
> .   .   .   .
> .   .   .   Do not weep, good fools,
>
> .   .   .   .
> .   .   .   this action I now go on
> Is for my better grace. Adieu, my lord,
> I never wish'd to see you sorry, now
> I trust I shall. My women, come, you have leave.
>> (2.1.116–24)

When Paulina brings the infant Perdita to Leontes at night, the entire scene becomes a drawn-out portrayal of the king's physical repulsion. Paulina's final speech points graphically to what must be happening onstage:

> I pray you do not push me, I'll be gone.
> Look to your babe, my lord, 'tis yours. Jove send her
> A better guiding spirit! What needs these hands?
> You, that are thus so tender o'er his follies,
> Will never do him good, not one of you.
> So, so. Farewell, we are gone.
>> (2.3.125–30)

Even the announcement of Mamillius's death is put in terms of withdrawal, departure:

SERVANT: O sir, I shall be hated to report it!
              The Prince your son, with mere conceit and
                 fear
              Of the Queen's speed, is gone.
LEONTES: How? gone?
SERVANT: Is dead.
                            (3.2.143–45)

In the tragic part of the play, all the Leontean scenes are presented in specific terms of "going." Not only does Leontes physically repel Hermione, Mamillius, Polixenes, Camillo, Paulina, Perdita, and Antigonus, he also seeks to disengage himself from the very ongoing nature of life. His is a cold spirit of negativism. Brooding like the winter on a procreative past that brought with life a knowledge of death—"when / Three crabbèd months had sour'd themselves to death" (1.2.102)—Leontes expresses his fear of time through hatred of sex, a hysterical misogyny, and obsessive threats of death.

The attitude toward sex is plain enough: "Go to, go to! / How she holds up the neb! the bill to him!" (1.2.182–83). One thinks of Lear's "The wren goes to't, and the small gilded fly / Does lecher in my sight" (4.6.112–13). For Leontes as well, the going-to of sex has become horribly repulsive; affection "stabs" and "infects," "revolted" wives are "sluiced" by paramours, the flax wench "puts to," his sheets are "spotted." But, unlike Lear, Leontes keeps his vision of sexual corruption within a relatively narrow focus; all the blame is heaped on women. Misogyny is his distinctive accent:

> women say so—
> That will say any thing. (1.2.130–31)

> O thou thing! (2.1.82)

> She's an adultress. (2.1.78)

> He dreads his wife. . . . a callat
> Of boundless tongue. (2.3.80, 91–92)

> I ne'er heard yet
> That any of these bolder vices wanted

> Less impudence to gainsay what they did
> Than to perform it first.
>
> (3.2.54–57)

Suiting the word to the action, he four times stands across from a woman whom he attacks for "going" and whom he then causes to "go" from the stage.

It is crucially important to realize that such sex-combat or rejection of women organizes the entire visual structure of the play's first half. Once we grasp the pattern, much that remains falls into place. Leontes' rejection of women accompanies his attempt to be self-sufficient, to protect his oft-mentioned "heart," to be the "center," and to found his "faith" only upon himself. He will not share the creative process with anyone else. He seeks to be the sole dispenser of life and death, to run the show:

> Is this nothing?
> Why then the world and all that's in't is nothing.
>
> (1.2.292–93)

> you may as well
> Forbid the sea for to obey the moon
> As or by oath remove or counsel shake
> The fabric of his folly, whose foundation
> Is pil'd upon his faith, and will continue
> The standing of his body.
>
> (1.2.426–31)

> if I mistake
> In those foundations which I build upon,
> The centre is not big enough to bear
> A schoolboy's top.
>
> (2.1.101–3)

> There is no truth at all i' th' oracle. (3.2.140)

Leontes' faith is founded where it should not be, in himself alone. When he denies the oracle, he openly presumes against the godhead, denies his created status. As king he has perhaps some reason to become trapped in divine analogy, but as man, dependent upon woman in order to play his part in creation, he cannot be self-sufficient. He cannot promise life by himself. He can only threaten death. And when he banishes woman, his becomes equally an idiom of death:

> give mine enemy a lasting wink. (1.2.317)

> Commit them to the fire! (2.3.96)

> The bastard brains with these my proper hands
> Shall I dash out.
>
> > (2.3.140–41)

> for the fail
> Of any point in't shall not only be
> Death to thyself but to thy lewd-tongu'd wife.
>
> > (2.3.170–72)

> Look for no less than death. (3.2.91)

Shakespeare's reduplicating structure thus forces the audience to hear and see, remember and anticipate, the one strikingly obsessive act on Leontes' part, that is, rejection and expulsion of women, kin, and company, together with threats of death. In many ways, Leontes shows himself caught in the quintessential winter's tale, enacting the title of the play, unable to see ahead to "this coming summer," looking back in anguish to a time when lambs frisked in the sun. He has become the lion in winter, old man winter, the character in Mamillius's story ("a sad tale's best for winter") who "dwelt by a church-yard" of graves. Our penultimate image of him in the tragic portion of the play is as a man caught in the deepest winter of despair. After announcing Hermione's death, Paulina, at least momentarily, denies Leontes the power of effective repentance:

> A thousand knees,
> Ten thousand years together, naked, fasting,
> Upon a barren mountain, and still winter
> In storm perpetual, could not move the gods
> To look that way thou wert.
>
> > (3.2.210–14)

Shakespeare's materializing imagination will immediately produce a wintry storm and present onstage the violent death of Antigonus.

An audience watching and weighing the four pulsations of madness outlined here should find, during a well-directed and well-acted performance, that Leontes' storm perpetual is regularly if briefly interrupted by a still small voice. All four of the king's scenes are crowded, loud, violent, rhetorically flamboyant. Each is self-fragmenting as exits are made away from Leontes. Hatred and death are the topics, fear and alienation the results. This deepening human winter is in essence the plot. But there is a counterplot.

The counterplot consists of the four relatively brief moments when Leontes is offstage. They are: (1) the conversation of Camillo and Archidamus in the first scene, (2) the meeting of Camillo and Polixenes at the end of the second scene together with the abbreviated tale of Mamillius at the beginning of the third scene, (3) Paulina at the prison in the fourth scene, and (4) the messengers returning from Delphos in the sixth scene. What the audience sees when Leontes is onstage is opposition leading to static isolation. What it sees when he is offstage is cooperation leading to the forward movement of a pair. Archidamus turns from fending off imagined accusations to agreeing with Camillo in the hopes of the young Mamillius; the two counsellors pass across the stage in final amity. After Leontes reveals his jealousy, Camillo meets Polixenes, and they decide to escape together. We see them pass across the stage as friends. Paulina, in the prison, gathers Emilia to her purpose and exits with her. Cleomenes and Dion marvel at their Delphic journey and hasten forward to court.

Leontes, like the last season of the year, appears to look back and view all the generative goings-on of life as repugnant and ineffectual delays against death: "go to," "go, play," "go, rot," "go," he says continually. The actors in the small, interstitial scenes are cast in a wholly different perspective. They look forward to *going* forward, and they grasp hopefully at generative continuity and renewal. Archidamus and Camillo forecast the great "going" of the play itself, the summer visit to Bohemia, and they see that the promise of youth freshens old hearts. Polixenes and Camillo find faith in each other by concentrating upon hereditary gentleness and honor, the regenerating opposites of that "hereditary imposition" noted earlier in the play. Polixenes speaks of "our parents' noble names, / In whose success we are gentle" (1.2.393–94). Camillo says: "by the honor of my parents, I / Have utt'red truth" (1.2.442–43), and Polixenes concludes: "Come, Camillo, / I will respect thee as a father, if / Thou bear'st my life off" (1.2.460–62). In the four brief scenes, the audience can hear brave and hopeful redefinitions of the human family. Not only do the counsellors take

physic from the prince and not only do the fleeing men find a
certain family identity or bond between themselves, but also Paulina
manages to absolve Perdita of inherited talent by stressing that she
shares the higher and more universal parentage of us all:

> You need not fear it, sir.
> This child was prisoner to the womb, and is
> By law and process of great Nature thence
> Freed and enfranchis'd.
>
> (2.2.56–59)

And, finally, as the little scenes take us further and further from
Leontes' court and closer to the journey of the play itself, we
experience a wider perspective upon the generative continuum that
binds us together. The messengers sense that they have journeyed
to the quick of nature: "The climate's delicate, the air most sweet, /
Fertile the isle" (3.1.1–2). Privileged to glance upward toward
higher powers and to hear the "voice o' th' oracle, / Kin to Jove's
thunder" (3.1.9–10), they gain intimations of a new birth in the
"event o' th' journey":

> When the oracle
> (Thus by Apollo's great divine seal'd up)
> Shall the contents discover, something rare
> Even then will rush to knowledge. Go; fresh horses!
> And gracious be the issue!
>
> (3.1.18–22)

This "going," unlike the goings that leave Leontes self-enclosed,
rushes toward hope of issue. The whole image is one of birth as the
seal gives way, the contents are discovered, and what is rare bursts
forth. All four of the non-Leontean scenes thus have to do with
accepting and indeed welcoming the progress of generation that
makes life ongoing. Carefully opposed and interposed, as they are,
against the blustering wrath of the king's scenes, these four moments invite the spectators to recall and anticipate a more sane
idiom of praise, prayer, and hope. In them it is hinted that the red
blood may someday reign in the winter's pale.

In the light of these scenic contrasts and their implications, we
can better understand the theatrical force of *The Winter's Tale* in its
tragic portion. The four scenes in which Leontes misdefines Hermione
or Paulina are all statue scenes. In each, he points an accusatory

finger at a woman, centrally observed, and charges her with artifice and deceit. Hermione "plays"; she hangs "like her medal" about Bohemia's neck. Leontes sees his wife in terms of an art object, like a statue, to be examined by bystanders: "You, my lords, / Look on her, mark her well" (2.1.64–65). He takes all for show: "Praise her but for this her without-door form" (2.1.69). He lives in a world of deceitful appearances. Earlier he had confessed: "I am angling," "I play too." Thinking of himself as "a very trick / For them to play at will" (2.1.51–52), he complains that others laugh at him and "make their pastime" at his sorrow. His scenes with Hermione and Paulina have a staged quality. He forgets his lines and responds as would an actor: "O, I am out" (2.1.72). He thinks that Paulina was "set on" by Antigonus. He refuses, in other words, to accord to either of these women any sincerity, or stable inward faith. Believing that all is artifice and play, he seizes the role of artificer and playmaker. The trial scene is intended to be his masterpiece; there too Hermione stands like a statue in central isolation. "My life stands in the level of your dreams" (3.2.81), she tells Leontes. It is a terrible truth. Leontes has become caught up in the nightmare of unfaith. To him, others lack reality; he thinks of them as being cold as dead men (2.1.151–52), past all shame (3.2.84). In the play's final scene, he will help to wake a statue, but now he treats the living woman as if she were sleeping marble. When Hermione swoons and appears to die, Paulina aptly challenges Leontes to see if he "can bring / Tincture or lustre in her lip, her eye, / Heat outwardly or breath within" (3.2.204–6). The king, of course, can perform no such creative act; indeed he himself sinks to a shamed and still impotence.

We think of Shakespeare primarily as a verbal artist, forgetting his amazing power to enthrall us with sheer pictographic debate. Leontes at first out-Herods Herod, rising through a crescendo of furious gestures, secretly and then openly denouncing Hermione, striding forward to taunt among the spectators "many a man" with cuckoldry, pointing Hermione offstage, forcing Paulina's exit, stalking around the infant Perdita, plucking Antigonus's beard, striking the oracle from the hand of his astonished officer.

Yet all this happens in a dream of disrelation. The spectators, who have witnessed and suffered under the four assaults of tyrannical madness, must long, surely, for counterviolence, for revenge. It comes, of course, swiftly and, as often, perhaps even too harshly.

When the panic-stricken messenger rushes in to shout that Mamillius is dead, when Hermione falls senseless, then Leontes halts in the very act of blaspheming Apollo and stands still at last, reduced now to silence, sculpted into the image of mortified man. And now the dialectical alternation of jealousy and trust is broken as Paulina begins to blast and purge the king's accumulated guilt. As Polixenes, on hearing of Leontes' suspicion, thought of Judas who "did betray the Best" (1.2.419), so Paulina tells Leontes: "thou betrayedst Polixenes" (3.2.185). It was a "damnable" act. That and the attempted corruption of Camillo were "trespasses." Even a "devil" would have repented before casting out Perdita. Following Leontes' contrast between Camillo's glistering "piety" and his own "black" deeds, Paulina's tirade (3.2.175–214) smacks of exorcism. Here is an energetic and sustained recognition of the king's madness and a convincing rejection of it as well, a theatrically impressive and satisfying purgation.

A sense of sacred purgation at the close of the trial scene is entirely appropriate. When Leontes asks pardon for his "great profaneness" against the oracle (3.2.154), we see that profaneness has been the overriding horror of the play. In *The Winter's Tale*, as in all the romances, Shakespeare shows the nothingness of life lived on the thin lateral line of the secular, where friendship and kinship may be thought to serve self-interest rather than the purposes of a higher order, "great creating nature." All the romances depict dramatic epiphanies when divine powers make themselves manifest and creatures on this worldly plane are reminded of the towering forces which intersect and influence their little linear lives. The halting steps which Leontes, with Paulina's help, now can take toward the "chapel" in furtherance of his penitential vows only hint at the vast journey to be taken by the play toward knowledge of a wide creation in which human love is seen to play its fruitful part. It will be a journey toward knowledge of "the gods themselves" in their full immanence and toward a capacity on all sides to respond when Paulina at last commands: "Is it requir'd / You do awake your faith" (5.3.94–95). But that journey, to be successful, must not be lightly undertaken, and it is the burden of the play's tragic portion to make its audience hunger for the community and comfort of awakening faith. Through the intensity of Leontes' angry doubt and the antithetical structuring of scenes playing that doubt off against nascent belief, Shakespeare has caused *The Winter's Tale* to carry its often painful but always instructive burden supremely well.

Leontes and the Spider: Language and Speaker in Shakespeare's Last Plays

Anne Barton

HERMIONE:	Come, sir, now
	I am for you again. Pray you sit by us,
	And tell's a tale.
MAMILLIUS:	Merry or sad shall't be?
HERMIONE:	As merry as you will.
MAMILLIUS:	A sad tale's best for winter. I have one
	Of sprites and goblins.
HERMIONE:	Let's have that, good sir.
	Come on, sit down; come on, and do your best
	To fright me with your sprites; you're powerful at it.
MAMILLIUS:	There was a man—
HERMIONE:	Nay, come, sit down; then on.
MAMILLIUS:	Dwelt by a churchyard—I will tell it softly;
	Yond crickets shall not hear it.
HERMIONE:	Come on then,
	And give't me in mine ear.
	[*Enter* LEONTES, ANTIGONUS, Lords *and* Others.]
LEONTES:	Was he met there? his train? Camillo with him?
I LORD:	Behind the tuft of pines I met them; never
	Saw I men scour so on their way. I eyed them
	Even to their ships.

From *Shakespeare's Styles: Essays in Honour of Kenneth Muir*, edited by Philip Edwards, Inga-Stina Ewbank, and G. K. Hunter. © 1980 by Cambridge University Press.

LEONTES: How blest am I
In my just censure, in my true opinion!
Alack, for lesser knowledge! How accursed
In being so blest! There may be in the cup
A spider steeped, and one may drink, depart,
And yet partake no venom, for his knowledge
Is not infected; but if one present
Th' abhorred ingredient to his eye, make
    known
How he hath drunk, he cracks his gorge, his
    sides,
With violent hefts. I have drunk, and seen
    the spider.
Camillo was his help in this, his pander.
There is a plot against my life, my crown;
All's true that is mistrusted. That false villain
Whom I employed was pre-employed by him;
He has discovered my design, and I
Remain a pinched thing; yea, a very trick
For them to play at will.
                                (*The Winter's Tale* 2.1.21–52)

The Winter's Tale begins where many of Shakespeare's earlier comedies had ended. Friendship, no longer love's rival, has found a
spacious if subordinate place for itself within the domain of marriage. Leontes enters the play with his wife Hermione and his friend
Polixenes: three people apparently in possession of that harmonious, adult relationship which the youthful protagonists of *Two
Gentlemen of Verona, Love's Labour's Lost, The Merchant of Venice,
Much Ado about Nothing* and *All's Well That Ends Well* had struggled
painfully, over five acts, to achieve. Mamillius and Florizel, the
children whose birth is predicated at the end of so many Shakespearian Comedies, actually exist. The story is, or should be, over.
So powerful is this sense of being in a place just beyond the normal
terminus of Shakespeare's comedies that, even at the beginning of
act 2, when Leontes has perversely begun to un-build his paradise,
it is possible to hear the echoes of another and less disturbing
winter's tale:

Now it is the time of night
That the graves, all gaping wide,

> Every one lets forth his sprite,
> In the church-way paths to glide.
> (*A Midsummer Night's Dream*
> 5.1.368–71)

Mamillius's whispered story "of sprites and goblins" will be as harmless as Puck's fifth-act account of the terrors of the night: a ghost story carefully qualified, in *A Midsummer Night's Dream*, by the final benediction of the fairies. Safe in her warm, domestic interior, Hermione listens indulgently to a child's tale of grave-yard horrors. Neither of them notices that, as in Peele's *The Old Wives' Tale*, someone has appeared on stage to tell Mamillius's tale for him. It is Leontes's story of the night, not Mamillius's, that the theatre audience actually hears, and this adult fantasy is neither harmless nor amusing.

Leontes, like Othello before him, asserts passionately that ignorance is bliss:

> I had been happy if the general camp,
> Pioneers and all, had tasted her sweet body,
> So I had nothing known.
> (*Othello* 3.3.349–51)

Othello's sophistical insistence that a man is robbed only if he knows he is had concentrated attention upon Othello himself: a man constitutionally incapable of existing—whether for good or ill—except in a state of certainty and total commitment. His false logic, engendered by the psychological pain of the moment, had been an unavailing attempt at self-delusion discredited by the speaker in the very moment of constructing it. Othello, in agony, deliberately plays with the idea of a blessed ignorance from which, through Iago's insinuations, he has effectively been debarred. He invents the gross "pioneers" as a form of self-torture, while trying simultaneously to persuade himself that paradise would not be lost even if he were the only man who still believed in it. But he knows that he cannot any longer believe.

Leontes' speech in *The Winter's Tale*, for all its superficial similarity, is very different from Othello's. The little, inset story of the spider is palpably an old wives' tale: a piece of unnatural natural history which Leontes trots out as part of his self-defeating effort to make something out of nothing, to give substance to a bad dream. As such, it functions in ways of which the speaker is himself unaware, tells a truth he consciously rejects. If Leontes sees himself as being in Othello's situation, we do not. Othello, with some excuse, could not distinguish between Desdemona's truth and Iago's cunning falsehood. He was not the only person in the play to make this mistake. Leontes, on the other hand, inhabits a world of clear-cut black and white, one in which there is no Iago, and even the herd of anonymous gentlemen at the court always know that Hermione is innocent. Leontes' mind, as his words involuntarily but quite explicitly inform us, has poisoned itself, breeding madness from an illusory evil, even as the minds of people doomed by voodoo or black magic are supposed to do. Whether visible or not, the spider in the cup is itself innocuous: it is the human imagination that is destructive and deadly. This is the most important thing Leontes has to tell us. It is characteristic, however, of the last plays, that the speaker should be quite unconscious of what, for the theatre audience, is the primary meaning of his own words.

In his earlier plays, Shakespeare had very occasionally anticipated this technique. Usually, he did so for straightforward comic effect—one thinks of the word "ass" as Dogberry indignantly applies it to himself, or as Bottom uses it, innocently, after his translation. Fools who luxuriate in words without understanding their proper meanings, as Dogberry does throughout *Much Ado about Nothing*, Touchstone's Audrey with the epithet "foul," or Cleopatra's clown (more profoundly) with the term "immortal," are given to making sense of a kind they would consciously repudiate. It is part of the character of the Hostess in the *Henry IV* plays that she should remain blithely unaware of the bawdy double entendres which other people detect in her speech, unintentional indecencies which tend to overbear her own meaning. Only in *Troilus and Cressida*, however, did Shakespeare exploit the device in ways that were, fundamentally, not comic. The play is conditioned throughout by the audience's foreknowledge of the fate of Troy, and of the destiny of each individual character. A unique and all-encompassing irony ensures that characters seldom speak out of their own, present moment of fictional time without an audience interpreting their words in the light of the myth as a whole. So, when Helen suggests languidly that "this love will undo us all" (3.1.103–4), what for her is mere badinage converts instantly into a sinister and alien truth. Pandarus regards it as a jocular impossibility that Cressida should ever be false to Troilus. Should his niece falter, "let all pitiful goers-between be called to the world's end after my name—call them all Pandars; let all constant men be Troiluses, all false women Cressids, and all brokers between Pandars. Say 'Amen' " (3.2.195–200). It is only for the audience, painfully aware that this is precisely the significance which these names now have, that "Amen" sticks in the throat.

   Troilus and Cressida is a special case. (Indeed, it is interesting that Shakespeare should have wished to stress the ineluctable end of the Troy story in this fashion, as he did not with what might have been regarded as the equally predetermined patterns of English history.) In general, the compulsion to drive a wedge between dramatic speech and the nature and intentions of the speaker becomes important only in his late plays. One must be careful, I think, not to confuse this late stylistic development with ordinary ambiguity—the shadowy penumbra of meanings, not necessarily in the control of the speaker, which may surround a given word. Nor is it the same as that kind of implicit, underlying irony which becomes visible only when a passage is analysed in the study, or remembered from the special vantage point of the fifth act. When Henry V, before Harfleur, exhorts his soldiers to imitate tigers, greyhounds, cannons, or pitiless granite escarpments, his words are a successful incitement to action. Only in the context of the whole play, and *after the dramatic moment is past*, leaving us to confront an immobile Bardolph and Pistol, is it possible to reflect that he is asking men to be both more and considerably less than human. Obviously, Henry himself does not see the terms he employs as equivocal, an impoverishment as well as an epic magnification. The point is that, in the theatre, neither do we. Or, at least, the speech as heard projects this sense in a way that is almost subliminal.

   Similarly, when Othello, in Cyprus, exclaims of Desdemona,

> Perdition catch my soul
> But I do love thee; and when I love thee not
> Chaos is come again,
>
> (3.3.91–93)

or Macbeth asserts, "Had I but died an hour before this chance, / I had lived a blessed time" (2.3.89–90), the literal but at this instant merely potential truth lurking behind the hyperbole is secondary to the meaning of the lines as the speaker intends them, but also as we hear them in the moment of utterance. Othello and Macbeth, like

Pandarus and Leontes, speak more truly than they know, but the
bitter prophecy inherent in their words—like the unwitting predic-
tions of Buckingham, Lady Anne, or Richard himself ("Myself
myself confound") in *Richard III*—will always be submerged in the
theatre by other and more immediately arresting considerations.
Even if one's mind does flicker forward to "the tragic loading of
this bed," here, in the particular stage-present of act 3, Othello's
lines make themselves felt essentially as Othello himself feels them:
as a spontaneous declaration of love and faith. Macbeth's cry, while
it certainly prefigures his fifth-act recognition of a life fallen irreme-
diably into the "sear, the yellow leaf," concentrates attention as it is
uttered upon the audacity of his dissembled horror. That is the
primary register.

   This is not, however, the way we react to Leontes' spider, or
to his assertion that "I / Play too; but so disgraced a part, whose
issue / Will hiss me to my grave" (1.2.187–89). Here, as in his
angry words to Hermione,

> Your actions are my dreams.
> You had a bastard by Polixenes,
> And I but dreamed it,
>
> (3.2.80–82)

it is what we take to be the *primary* meaning of the speech which is
concealed from the speaker. In the last example, Leontes' heavy
irony functions, for us, as a simple statement of truth. This is also
true of the convoluted reasoning through which he persuaded himself, in act 1, that because "affection" may communicate with
dreams, be coactive with the unreal, and because it "fellow'st
nothing" (1.2.38–46), it may conjoin with "something"—and has.
It is interesting to compare the false logic here with Brutus's
soliloquy in the orchard in *Julius Caesar*: "Then, lest he may,
prevent" (2.1.28). All of the passages from *The Winter's Tale* are
entirely and almost impersonally apt as descriptions of the dramatic
situation as we, but not Leontes, apprehend it. Mirrors of action
almost more than of character, they do not focus attention upon
Leontes' central self in the way that Othello's and Brutus's assertions had illuminated the needs and complexities of their natures.

   A number of critics have felt that Shakespeare, in his last plays,
destroyed that close relationship between language and dramatic
character which had seemed the permanent achievement of his

maturity. Charles Olson observed in 1950 that the later Shakespeare "very much doesn't any longer bother to keep his music and thought inside the skin of the person and situation, able as he had been to make each person of his play make his or her individual self register its experience of reality." James Sutherland, confronting the opening lines of *Cymbeline*, suspected that "the person who is thinking rapidly, breaking off, making fresh starts and so on, is not the character, but Shakespeare himself." For Sutherland, this dislocation between verse and character reflected a Shakespeare who, if not exactly "bored" (Strachey's epithet), was at least a little jaded: a man to whom poetry no longer came as naturally as leaves to a tree, who had to force himself now to create at all, and had taken to writing in a strained and entirely cerebral way. S. L. Bethell also claimed that the twisted rhythms and tortured syntax of the last plays represented "Shakespeare's mind, not the character's; indeed, it draws our attention *away from* the speaker to what is spoken about." Unlike Sutherland, Bethell approved of what seemed to him a new technique designed to give prominence to those metaphysical truths which alone could justify Shakespeare's use of plot material so naïve and silly. More recently, Hallett Smith has shifted the emphasis away from Shakespeare himself to the nature of the stage action. "It is noteworthy," he says of certain passages in *Cymbeline* and *The Winter's Tale*, "that the speeches do not so much characterize the speaker as dramatize the occasion."

Smith appears to me to have come closest to the truth. It is not easy to see why a dramatist who had so triumphantly solved what Daniel Seltzer describes as "the problem of causing verbal expression to spring naturally from the inner life of the stage personality," who had developed "a technique uniquely Shakespearian: that of expression, moment by moment, of an inner state and an immediate present time," should suddenly decide to sacrifice the accomplishment. But then it is not easy, either, to understand the logic which impelled Michelangelo to forget everything he had painfully learned about the realistic articulation of the human body and return, in the Rondanini *Pietà*, to the stiff, non-naturalistic forms of Romanesque art. For whatever reason, Shakespeare at the end of his writing life chose to subordinate character to action in ways that seem to give Aristotle's conviction of the necessary primacy of the μῦθος a new twist.

Editors of *The Tempest* have often wished to transfer Miranda's verbal assault upon Caliban in act 1 ("Abhorrèd slave, / Which any print of goodness wilt not take") to Prospero. It seems almost inconceivable that her innocence and gentleness should be capable of such rugged and uncompromising vituperation. Examination of the last plays as a group, however, tends to suggest that the Folio is correct. Over and over again, Shakespeare jettisons consistency of characterisation because he is more interested in the impersonal quality of a moment of dramatic time. This is what happens near the beginning of act 3 of *The Tempest*, when Miranda somewhat startlingly produces the image of a concealed pregnancy as the means of declaring her love to Ferdinand: "And all the more it seeks to hide itself, / The bigger bulk it shows" (3.1.80–81). That Ophelia, in her madness, should reveal that she has secretly committed to memory all the verses of a rude song about St. Valentine's Day, certainly says something about Ophelia, and about the pathos of her attempts to look in directions sternly prohibited by Polonius and Laertes. It would obviously be inappropriate and futile to apply the same reasoning to Miranda's lines. They are there, not to tell us anything about sexual repression on the island, but because—as the betrothal masque will later make even more plain—Shakespeare is concerned, above all, to delineate this marriage in terms of natural fertility and increase. Even so, Miranda says to Caliban earlier what the situation, as opposed to maidenly decorum and the pliability of her own nature, would seem to demand.

Miranda is not the only heroine to be treated in this fashion in the late plays. As early as *Pericles*, Marina had anticipated Miranda's confrontation with Caliban in the uncharacteristic venom and masculinity of her reproof of Boult:

> Thou art the damned doorkeeper to every
> Coistrel that comes inquiring for his Tib;
> To the choleric fisting of every rogue
> Thy ear is liable; thy food is such
> As hath been belched on by infected lungs.
> (4.6.163–67)

The lines, however well suited to the Duke in *Measure for Measure*, are not easy for an actress to encompass, considering that she will have spent most of her previous scenes epitomising a kind of gentle and melancholy lyricism, coupled with an innocence incapable of even understanding the Bawd's professional instructions (4.2.116–23). One previous abrupt departure from Marina's normal manner, during her account to Leonine of the sea-storm of her birth (4.1.61–66), has at least warned the performer what to expect. In both passages, Shakespeare appears to be using Marina less as a character than as a kind of medium, through which the voice of the situation can be made to speak.

Further instances of this attitude towards dramatic speech may be found most readily by turning to those passages in the late plays which, for one reason or another, have aroused critical censure or disagreement. Dr Johnson found the third-act soliloquy of Belarius in *Cymbeline* ("These boys know little they are sons to th' King") positively exasperating in its irrationality and unabashed expository purpose. Belarius is not, elsewhere, so crudely confiding, like a character in an old play. The improbability, however, of the story he has to tell has already been admitted by Shakespeare, indeed brought to our attention, in the opening dialogue between the first and second gentlemen (1.1.57–67). Belarius's speech in act 3 reflects, not his own personality or feelings at the moment (elsewhere clearly enough defined), but simply the character of the events he describes: remote, fantastic, and overtly artificial. The same will be true of the highly wrought and convoluted prose in which the courtiers recount the finding of Perdita in *The Winter's Tale*, as it is of Iachimo's insistence, at the end of *Cymbeline*, upon transforming what ought to be an agonised confession of guilt into an intricate and palpable work of fiction. Iachimo's flowery and long-winded account of how Posthumus was led to wager on Imogen's chastity bears little resemblance to the episode we actually saw, back in the fourth scene of act 1. The gentlemen were not, as Iachimo claims they were, sitting at a feast praising their loves of Italy, until their hyperbole stung the melancholy Posthumus into a celebration of his wife, and then into accepting Iachimo's trial. The reality was different, and more complex than this. Iachimo has tidied it all up, brought it closer—both stylistically and in terms of fact—to a romance world. He does this for reasons which (again) have less to do with his character than with the way *Cymbeline*, in its final scene, deliberately treats its plot material as unreal.

A similar concern to express situation before character allows the wicked Queen in *Cymbeline* to speak of Britain in words that would not misbecome John of Gaunt, when she proudly refuses to pay the Roman tribute. Even Cloten, when he announces that "Britain is / A world by itself," can expect applause (3.1.12–13). Arviragus appears to wander off the point in ways of which true grief, even in a verse play, ought to be incapable when he assures the "dead" Fidele of the kindly attentions of the ruddock's "charitable bill—O bill, sore shaming / Those rich-left heirs that let their fathers lie / Without a monument" (4.2.226–28). His brother Guiderius reproves him for playing "in wench-like words with that / Which is so serious." It is Arviragus, however, who is unconsciously faithful to the quality of the situation: Fidele is not dead, but merely asleep, as the result of the Queen's potion. It is interesting to compare Arviragus's lament here with the comic frenzy of the Nurse when she discovers Juliet "dead" on her wedding day. Like Fidele, Juliet is only drugged into a semblance of death and, in this sense, the Nurse's ludicrous attempts at tragic style ("O day! O day! O day! O hateful day"; 4.5.52) are entirely appropriate to a situation which is not what it seems to be. With the Nurse, however, one is aware first and foremost of how perfectly *in character* her lamentations are. Presumably, she sounded much the same when poor Susan went to God. This is not true of Arviragus's elegy in *Cymbeline*, a speech which, if anything, seems oddly hard to square with what we know about this princely rustic.

At least two notorious problems in the last plays may result from Shakespeare's use of this dramatic technique. It is always hard to know what to make of Lysimachus's asseveration to Marina, at the end of their interview in the brothel, that he came "with no ill intent; for to me / The very doors and windows savour vilely" (4.6.108–9). He has certainly created the impression, in the scene as a whole, that he is a man perfectly at home in a house of prostitution, and intimately acquainted with its ways. "How now! How a dozen of virginities?" As the Bawd remarks, "Your Honour knows what 'tis to say well enough" (4.6.19, 31). There is not the slightest hint that the Governor of Mytilene may be dissembling. Is his explanation to Marina a desperate attempt to save face before he too, with the other converts, goes off to "hear the vestals sing"? Or is the answer simply that Shakespeare is not interested in Lysimachus's motivation: during the dialogue with the professionals, and with Marina, he is a young man of rank in search of a sound whore, because that is what the situation demands. Afterwards, he is not— because he is going to marry Marina. Something similar seems to be happening with Paulina's outburst to Leontes after the "death" of Hermione.

> I say she's dead; I'll swear't. If word nor oath
> Prevail not, go and see. If you can bring
> Tincture or lustre in her lip, her eye,
> Heat outwardly or breath within, I'll serve you
> As I would do the gods. But, O thou tyrant!
> Do not repent these things, for they are heavier
> Than all thy woes can stir; therefore betake thee
> To nothing but despair. A thousand knees
> Ten thousand years together, naked, fasting,
> Upon a barren mountain, and still winter
> In storm perpetual, could not move the gods
> To look that way thou wert.
>
> (*The Winter's Tale* 3.2.200–211)

Paulina, of course, is lying—or, at least, she seems to be from the vantage point of the fifth act. In the scene itself, one must assume that she is a woman half crazed with shock and grief, expressing the truth of the situation. For the theatre audience at this point in the play, Hermione, unlike Fidele, is indeed dead. Paulina's voice is faithful to the action. And it is characteristic of the last plays that Shakespeare should not bother, amid the partial revelations of the final scene, to provide any explanation of her previous behaviour.

Never a man who paid much attention to the requirements of neoclassical decorum when constructing character, the Shakespeare of the late plays seems to have abandoned even the basic convention by which, earlier, his servants and lower-class characters generally expressed themselves in homely, colloquial, if vivid, prose. The gardeners of *Richard II*, in their one, brief appearance, had been striking exceptions to this rule: emblematic, verse-speaking custodians of a garden more symbolic than literal and, as such, very different from Launce or Speed, Costard, the citizenry of the Roman plays, Cade's rabble, the Dromios, Grumio, Peter, Pompey, or the carriers at Rochester. Posthumus, on the other hand, is a humble, private gentleman but he has mysteriously acquired, in Pisanio, a servant of quite extraordinary verbal sophistication, who can tell Imogen to

> Forget that rarest treasure of your cheek,
> Exposing it—but, O, the harder heart!
> Alack, no remedy!—to the greedy touch
> Of common-kissing Titan, and forget
> Your laboursome and dainty trims wherein
> You made great Juno angry.
>
> (3.4.159–64)

Even the gaoler in *Cymbeline*, although he speaks prose, seems (like Perdita herself, though without the justification of her lineage) to smack of something greater than himself, "too noble for this place." To place his meditation on death ("O, the charity of a penny cord"; 5.4.156–207) beside that of the grave-digger in *Hamlet* is to see how little Shakespeare is concerned, now, with any attempt at social realism. Even the Old Shepherd of *The Winter's Tale*, and the fishermen Patchbreech and Pilch in *Pericles*, seem to dodge in and out of their status-defined, comic roles in ways for which there are no real parallels in earlier plays. Stephano and Trinculo, in *The Tempest*, do not do this: they are consistently (and relatively realistically) conceived throughout. Shakespeare's orthodox handling of them, however, only serves to throw into relief the inexplicably civilised verse (if not the sentiments) of Caliban.

It is a commonplace of criticism to separate Imogen from the other young heroines of the last plays, to see her as a sister of Rosalind, Viola, Portia, or the Julia of *Two Gentlemen of Verona*, a character existing somewhat uncomfortably in a romance world not really designed to accommodate her. There is obviously some truth in this judgement, at least when Imogen is measured against Marina, Perdita, and Miranda. She does indeed seem to be more vigorous, complex, and three-dimensional than they, to summon up memories of the earlier heroines. And yet, when Cymbeline, at the very end, recognises "the tune of Imogen" (5.5.239), it is not easy to define just what he means. Unlike Rosalind or Viola, Imogen has seemed to manifest herself in several, divergent modes: passionate and chilly, timorous and aggressive, sometimes intensely feminine, sometimes not. This is partly the result of the way she submerges her own personality within that of the fictional Fidele, losing herself in her role, as Rosalind had not when she impersonated Ganymede, or Viola when she acted Cesario. Rosalind's mercurial, feminine self always shines through Ganymede, making

Orlando's acceptance of the wooing game credible. Viola constantly reminds us, as she talks to Orsino, Feste, and Olivia, or struggles to overcome her physical cowardice when confronting Aguecheek, of the lonely, isolated girl she really is. The image is curiously double. In the theatre, an audience remains aware that Fidele is really Imogen. Yet her identity is overlaid by another: that of the "boy" whom Guiderius, Arviragus, Belarius and (later) Lucius see. We share their viewpoint, as we never share Olivia's, Orlando's, or Orsino's. This is not because Imogen is particularly skilled at dissembling—indeed, the bluntness and impatient candour of her behaviour at court during the early scenes suggest precisely the opposite—but because Shakespeare has transformed her so completely, in her dialogue with other characters, into the person she is pretending to be, that we intermittently lose sight of the reality. It is possible that the page Fidele's lament for his dead master,

> Alas!
> There is no more such masters. I may wander
> From east to occident; cry out for service;
> Try many, all good; serve truly; never
> Find such another master
>
> (4.2.371–75)

made an imaginary situation seem so convincing that Shakespeare was impelled to introduce the subsequent aside (ll. 378–80) in order to remind us of the truth.

Shakespeare's handling of Imogen's disguise would seem to be a further example of the subordination, in the last plays, of character to the demands of stage action. It is also part of a new, and sometimes perplexing, attitude towards disguise and deceit generally. Pastoral Bohemia is a land in which ballad stories so improbable that they are virtual synonyms for fiction can eagerly be swallowed as true. There, no one sees through the various disguises of Autolycus, Florizel, Polixenes and Camillo. Elsewhere, however, dissembling and deceit tend to be transparent as they were not in earlier plays. "Here comes the Lord Lysimachus disguised," the Bawd remarks calmly in the fourth act of *Pericles* (4.6.16). One almost wonders why he troubled. When one considers how complex and vital an issue it had been in earlier plays—both the comedies and tragedies— to distinguish truth from falsehood, seeming from reality, how difficult to arrive in particular cases at Hamlet's understanding that "one may smile, and smile, and be a villain," the sudden diminution or disappearance of this problem from the last plays is startling. It would seem, however, to be to a considerable extent responsible for their special character and flavour.

Where Bassanio had agonised long over the riddle of the caskets at Belmont, Pericles solves Antiochus's conundrum without effort and at once. Later, at Pentapolis, his rusty armour and dejected manner fail to conceal his innate nobility and worth from King Simonides and his daughter. Both are eager, before they know his identity, to press this seemingly unequal marriage. Lysimachus stands more upon his dignity, but even he requires only the assurance of a birth certificate to offer his hand to the girl he met first in the stews. At Cymbeline's court, everyone but the king himself can see clearly that the queen is evil and not to be trusted, and also that Cloten is a boor, and the lowly Posthumus the only man worthy of such a jewel as Imogen. Courts are not usually so perceptive. Cornelius will not give the queen the poisons for which she asks. Pisanio will neither betray Posthumus by entering the service of Cloten, nor believe Posthumus when he brands Imogen as unchaste. Imogen herself sees through Iachimo's slander of Posthumus. Guiderius and Arviragus know, although they cannot explain why, that Fidele is akin to them as Belarius is not.

In *The Winter's Tale*, although Antigonus misinterprets a dream (and pays heavily for it), Leontes is really the only person who believes in Hermione's guilt. Everyone else, including the nameless gentlemen of the court, sees clearly that he is deluded. Camillo tells Leontes to dissemble with Polixenes: "with a countenance as clear / As friendship wears at feasts, keep with Bohemia" (1.2.343–44), and the king accepts his advice. "I will seem friendly, as thou hast advised me." Just how successful this attempt is emerges at the end of the act, when Polixenes assures Camillo that "I do believe thee: / I saw his heart in's face" (1.2.446–47). Duncan had lamented that "there's no art / To find the mind's construction in the face" (*Macbeth* 1.4.11–12), but in the last plays it seems to be true more often that no art is required: faces tell all, even when, as in the case of Leontes, their owners are making strenuous attempts at hypocrisy. Prospero, through his magic art, understands the true nature of everyone on the island. The knowledge adds doubtfully to his happiness. It contributes, however, to the general sense in this, as in the other romances, that the real problem, now, is not one of distinguishing good from evil but of deciding what to do with a knowledge which often seems to be acquired involuntarily rather than through any conscious effort at discrimination.

The involuntary plays a significantly new part in the last plays. Although, in general, good and evil are oddly transparent and recognisable for what they are, a few individual characters are arbitrarily deprived of this knowledge. Sealed off from everyone around them, they inhabit a strange, isolated state of consciousness in which they not only make false judgements, but cannot be reached or reasoned with by anyone else. These extreme states of mind are not arrived at, as it seems, by any logical, or psychologically comprehensible, process: they are simply "caught," like the 'flu. This happens to Pericles towards the end of the play. He appears in act 5 as a living dead man, one who has not spoken to anyone for three months. Only Marina can break through the barrier, and even she comes close to being defeated by the task. In the case of King Cymbeline, his delusion has come upon him before the beginning of the play, an inexplicable blindness which prevents him from seeing what is apparent to everyone else. Only the death of the wicked queen releases him from the spell. *The Tempest* stands slightly apart from the other romances, in that the trance which enwraps Alonso, Antonio, and Sebastian after the enchanted banquet is directly attributable to Prospero's art. Again, however, it has the effect of creating a distinction between a special, almost somnambulist state and a waking world of preternatural clarity and moral definition. Posthumus, in *Cymbeline*, shuts himself off from the light in act 2. Philario is a minor character, and he has never met Imogen, but even he can see that Iachimo's tale "is not strong enough to be believed / Of one persuaded well of" (2.4.131–32). Posthumus, however, has suddenly entered the troll kingdom of *Peer Gynt*, and no longer sees the world with the eyes of other men.

The madness of Leontes would seem to be generically like that of Pericles, Cymbeline, Posthumus and (with reservations) the three men of sin in *The Tempest*. But Shakespeare allows us to watch its inception and development at much greater length, a privilege which only serves to make the affliction itself more mysterious. Leontes comes to believe that he is the only person in Sicily capable of distinguishing truth from falsehood. In fact, he is the only person who cannot. What he describes, in the speech about the spider and the cup, as "my true opinion" is a chimera, a self-deception of the grossest kind. And indeed, only a few lines later, he is repeating this talismanic word *true* in a sentence which means one thing to him and, as so often, something quite different to the audience: "All's true that is mistrusted." Editors of *The Winter's Tale* tend to feel that the phrase is sufficiently obscure to require a gloss. They explain carefully that Leontes is justifying the truth of his own suspicions about Hermione and Polixenes—and so he is. The word order, on the other hand, is oddly convoluted. (Compare Ford's superficially similar statement in a similar situation in *The Merry Wives of Windsor*: "my intelligence is true; my jealousy is reasonable"; 4.2.130–32). *The Winter's Tale* inversion draws attention to a rival, and even more important, interpretation. What Leontes is telling us, without being aware that he does so, is that everything he thinks false is, in fact, true.

Throughout his writing life, Shakespeare displayed a marked predilection for analysing situations by way of contraries or antitheses. Dualities and polar opposites are a striking feature of his style, superimposed upon the individual verbal habits of particular characters: darkness and light, frost and fire, summer and winter, love and hate. Elizabethans, trained as they were in the discipline of formal rhetoric, often thought in such patterns. With Shakespeare, however, certain words seem to summon up their opposites almost automatically, as the result of an ingrained habit of mind almost more than from the requirements of a particular situation or rhetorical pattern. This is the case especially with the true–false antithesis, as even a quick glance at the two words in the Shakespeare concordance will reveal. They are surprisingly constant companions. In the last plays, however, something odd seems to happen to antithesis generally, and to the true–false figure in particular.

"Metaphysical" is a term frequently invoked to describe the stylistic peculiarities of the romances. And indeed, there is much to be said for using it, in Dr Johnson's sense of heterogeneous ideas yoked together by violence, analogies so ingenious it seems a wonder they were ever found at all. Characteristic of all four plays, but of *The Winter's Tale* in particular, is a form of similitude, usually employing the conjunction *as*, in which antithesis is employed to define resemblance in a fashion both unexpected and only superficially logical. When Antonio wants to assure Sebastian that Ferdinand is surely dead, he complicates a fundamentally simple assertion by explaining that " 'Tis as impossible that he's undrowned / As he that sleeps here swims" (2.1.228–29). Time, in *The Winter's Tale*, warns the theatre audience that he will "make stale / The glistering of this present, as my tale / Now seems to it" (4.1.13–15). Hermione is sure that her past life "hath been as continent, as chaste, as true, / As I am now unhappy" (3.2.31–33), and Paulina informs Leontes that she is "no less honest / Than you are mad" (2.2.70–71). Iachimo, purloining the sleeping Imogen's bracelet, finds it "as slippery as the Gordian knot was hard" (2.2.34). There are many other instances. In all of them, a negative and a positive statement are oddly conjoined. Moreover, although the syntax often appears to be setting up a clear-cut polarity (honest–dishonest, chaste–falsely accused), in fact the figure slides off into the oblique. The terms compared are not really antithetical: they are merely *different* in a way that makes one wonder why these particular instances have been made to confront each other at all.

The words *false* and *true* continue, in the last plays, to evoke one another, but Shakespeare tends to treat them, now, in an almost vertiginous way. Earlier true–false antitheses (e.g., "As false, by heaven, as heaven itself is true"; *Richard II* 4.1.64) had been clear cut. Although the complications attendant upon broken vows produced, in *Love's Labour's Lost* and *King John*, three isolated examples prophetic of the future, it is only in the romances that truth and falsehood come to engage habitually in a balancing act in which, at one and the same time, they remain polarities and seem to exchange identities. In the light of similar passages in *Cymbeline* and *The Winter's Tale*, Pericles's meditation on Antiochus at the beginning of the play sounds like an authentic and uncorrupted piece of Shakespearian text:

> If it be true that I interpret false,
> Then were it certain you were not so bad
> As with foul incest to abuse your soul.
> (1.1.124–26)

Even so, Cornelius, when deceiving Cymbeline's queen about the nature of the drug he gives her, describes himself as "the truer / So to be false with her" (1.5.43–44). Pisanio performs the same gyration in act 3, when he informs the absent Cloten that "true to thee / Were to prove false, which I will never be, / To him that is most true" (3.5.157–59), and reiterates the paradox in act 4: "Wherein I am false I am honest; not true to be true" (4.3.42). Leontes argues that even if women were as false as "o'er-dyed blacks," as water, wind or dice, "yet were it true / To say this boy were like me" (1.2.134–35).

Imogen's anguished investigation of what it means "to be false" extends the exercise:

> True honest men being heard, like false Aeneas,
> Were, in his time, thought false; and Sinon's weeping
> Did scandal many a holy tear, took pity
> From most true wretchedness. So thou, Posthumus,
> Wilt lay the leaven on all proper men:
> Goodly and gallant shall be false and perjured
> From thy great fail.
>
> (3.4.56–62)

Hermione on trial sees the same problem from the opposite side, but she delineates it in similar terms:

> Since what I am to say must be but that
> Which contradicts my accusation, and
> The testimony on my part no other
> But what comes from myself, it shall scarce boot me
> To say "Not guilty." Mine integrity
> Being counted falsehood shall, as I express it,
> Be so received.
>
> (3.2.20–26)

The pessimism of both women is unwarranted. Except for characters like Leontes and Posthumus, who have suddenly and arbitrarily gone blind, distinguishing between falsehood and truth as *moral* entities is no longer difficult. All of these riddling passages remind us of this fact. At the same time, they suggest, in their deliberate confounding of opposites, the presence of another kind of true–false confusion: one which is central to these plays.

On the whole, efforts to distinguish the fictional from the "real," art from life, tales from truth, come in the romances to replace the older, moral concern with identifying hypocrisy and deceit. It is not easy for characters to make these distinctions—nor, in some cases, for the theatre audience. Leontes, when he applies the story of the spider in the cup, mistakes a fiction of his own devising for fact, with disastrous results. He forces the imaginary to become true, even as Antonio does before *The Tempest* begins, when

> having into truth, by telling of it,
> Made such a sinner of his memory,
> To credit his own lie—he did believe
> He was indeed the Duke.
>
> (1.2.100–103)

Both of these are false and destructive fictions, credited only by their creators. And in both plays they can be countered only by another, and benevolent, kind of illusion: Prospero's restorative art, or the pastoral make-believe of Bohemia.

In Bohemia, almost all the special techniques of the last plays with which this essay has been concerned are on view simultaneously. People are constantly expressing the truth of the situation without grasping what, for us, is the primary meaning of their own words—as in the reiterated description of the lowly Perdita as a "queen." It has often been remarked that Polixenes and Perdita, in their debate on Art and Nature, perversely argue against their own position and intentions as they understand them at this point. Polixenes, after all, has come to the sheep-shearing precisely in order to prevent his gentle scion from grafting himself onto wild stock. Perdita, for her part, intends to make just such an "unnatural" marriage. Their words, inconsistent with the purpose of the two speakers, focus attention not upon them but upon the real nature of the situation.

Perdita dislikes acting as much as she dislikes nature's bastards in her rustic garden. It worries her that her own identity should be submerged so completely in that of the festival queen she plays, that her robes should change her disposition. In fact, she does lose herself in her part, even as Imogen had in that of Fidele, although in this case the scene in which she distributes the flowers seems to operate as a healing counterbalance to the earlier "play" in which her father, another unwilling actor, had fancied himself hissed off the stage in the role of cuckold. It is with great reluctance that Perdita agrees to continue in her royal part after Polixenes has revealed himself. Camillo's counsel to her to "disliken / The truth of your own seeming" (4.4.642–43) not only brings truth and falsehood into a linguistically dizzying relationship, in the manner characteristic of these plays; it expresses a truth beyond Camillo's ken. Like Imogen, Perdita must consent to "disguise / That which t'appear itself must not yet be / But by self-danger" (*Cymbeline* 3.4.143–45).

Autolycus, a man of various and willing disguises, may seem at first sight to be a hypocrite and dissembler in the manner of earlier plays. His real association, however, is with fictions rather than with genuine evil. Certainly his decision not to take the obviously profitable step of acquainting Polixenes with Florizel's intended flight—because to do so would be an honest action, and Autolycus prefers to remain true to his own falsehood—is scarcely that of a man whose villainy we can take seriously. At the end of the play, the Clown, his chief victim, is cheerfully defending his oath that Autolycus is "as honest a true fellow as any is in Bohemia" on the grounds that "if it be ne'er so false, a true gentleman may swear it in the behalf of his friend" (5.2.150–51, 156–58). Justice Shallow's man Davy, pleading for the notorious Visor because "the knave is mine honest friend" (2 *Henry IV* 5.1.47–48), never confounded the moral connotations of "knave" and "honest," despite his concern to mitigate the pejorative side. The Clown, on the other hand, calls precisely this polarity into doubt in ways that make it impossible for us to regard Autolycus as anything but what he is: a creator of fictions who, by not betraying Florizel to Polixenes, and by inventing a tale which frightens the Old Shepherd and the Clown into Sicily with the all-important fardel, is in fact the agent of the happy ending.

In Bohemia, people constantly confuse fact with fiction. Mopsa and Dorcas are almost obsessive in their desire to be assured that the pedlar's fantastic ballads are true. Their naïveté is comic and yet, later in the play, we find ourselves humbly sharing their impulse. The second gentleman announces that "such a deal of wonder is broken out within this hour that ballad-makers cannot be able to express it" (5.1.23–25). The preservation of Perdita and her reunion with her father are, as Shakespeare continually reminds us, "like an old tale," more improbable even than Autolycus's ballads. It is, however, a story that we too, in reading or watching the play, want to believe. This is even more true with the awakening of Hermione from marble to flesh, a resurrection which is as much a miracle for the theatre audience as for the characters involved. "It is required," Paulina says, "you do awake your faith" (5.3.94–95). What kind of faith?

Several kinds of fiction, as it seems, have operated in *The Winter's Tale*. The comedy ending which was the original point of departure dissolved almost at once into a dark tale of sprites and goblins. Then, it metamorphosed into a traditional comedy plot. Florizel and Perdita stand together in the last moments of the play as lovers who have won through, despite parental opposition and mistakes about identity, in the immemorial way of comedy. It is true that there is something they lack. Mamillius ought to be standing beside them: Florizel's friend, as Polixenes was Leontes'. But Mamillius, like Antigonus, is dead. Hermione, too, is wrinkled and older after the passing of sixteen years. Leontes does not get back exactly what he threw away. Still, he gets back far more than men can realistically expect. *The Winter's Tale* admits something that Shakespeare's Elizabethan comedies had tried to deny: happy endings are a fiction. A fiction, but not quite a fairy-tale.

Paulina declares of Hermione in the last scene:

> That she is living,
> *Were it but told you*, should be hooted at
> Like an old tale; but it *appears* she lives.
> (5.3.115–17: my italics)

The words are true, once again, in a way not comprehended by the speaker. It is, after all, because of the dramatic form in which this implausible fiction has been embodied, because of our complex, theatrical experience of this μῦθος, that we can give *The Winter's Tale* a kind of assent we deny to Greene's *Pandosto*. In the world as we know it, the dead do not return. Lost children generally stay lost, and shepherds' daughters do not attract the sons of kings. Ageing widows are not married off quite so neatly as Paulina. Shakespeare not only does not try to conceal, he positively emphasises the fact that his material is the archetypal stuff of legend and fairy-tale. That we respond to it as something far more powerful and engaging than *Cinderella* or *Beauty and the Beast* testifies to the subtlety with which Shakespeare has adjusted his language and dramatic art to the demands of a new mode: one in which plot, on the whole, has become more vivid and emotionally charged than character. And also, to a desperate artistic honesty which could admit, now, to creating fictions, while making us understand why and how much we should like those fictions to be real.

Shakespeare's Humanist Enterprise: The Winter's Tale

Louis L. Martz

The Winter's Tale begins to move within the context of Renaissance humanism through the striking process of "Atticizing" that Shakespeare performed in adapting material from Greene's *Pandosto*. First of all, he reverses the geographical location of the scenes, thus giving greater prominence to Sicilia, as opposed to Bohemia; in Greene's romance King Pandosto (Leontes) is King of Bohemia, not Sicilia. Having chosen to anchor his action in ancient Sicilia, that prosperous Greek colony, Shakespeare is not content to use Greene's curious conglomeration of names for his characters—some sounding Italian, some Latin, one Gothic, only a few really Greek. Instead, he seems to have recalled from North's Plutarch certain appropriate Greek (or Greek-like) names for his characters: Leontes, Antigonus, Cleomenes, Dion, Polyxemus (Polixenes?), Archidamus, Autolycus, Hermione, and Aemylia are all there. Two courtiers in Greene's romance named Franion and Capnio are merged into the figure of Camillo, the Italianate version of Camillus, name of a legendary hero in Plutarch. Garinter, the young son, becomes Mamillius. Greene's maiden, Fawnia, has a name that may suggest a Greek faun—but with overtones of lust hardly appropriate to the Perdita we know.

One might wonder why the perfectly good Greek name Egistus has been changed to the unusual name Polixenes, but it seems likely that the name Egistus is much too reminiscent of the villain of the

From *English Renaissance Studies: Presented to Dame Helen Gardner in Honour of Her Seventieth Birthday*. © 1980 by Oxford University Press. Clarendon, 1980.

123

Agamemnon story. Likewise the name Dorastus might seem to be more appropriate to the classical setting than the name Florizel, but this name is spoken very seldom in the play itself: throughout the pastoral scene in Bohemia the young prince is called by the splendid Greek name Doricles. At the same time Shakespeare increases the Greek atmosphere by adding two characters with striking Greek names, Cleomenes and Dion, as his two ambassadors to Apollo's oracle on "Delphos," replacing the six anonymous noblemen dispatched on this mission by Pandosto.

Then Shakespeare proceeds to introduce a scene (3.1) for which there is no exact precedent in Greene: the brief but beautiful glimpse of Cleomenes and Dion returning from the isle of "Delphos," with their awe-stricken and exalted memories of the island and its ceremonies sacred to "Great Apollo." Shakespeare is following Greene in naming the isle Delphos, a conception that seems to fuse Delphi and Delos. But there is nothing unlearned or ignorant about Shakespeare's usage of that name: it was common in Shakespeare's day. The fusion of names indeed works to very good effect, for more and more we come to realize that Apollo is the presiding deity of this play. Thus it is appropriate to have this allusion to the oracle visited by Aeneas at Apollo's chief sanctuary and birthplace, Delos, where Apollo was for centuries honoured by songs, dances, and games in a great festival where people gathered from all the Aegean isles and shores, as we know from the Homeric Hymn to Delian Apollo:

> in Delos do you most delight your heart; for there the long robed Ionians gather in your honour with their children and shy wives: mindful they delight you with boxing and dancing and song, so often as they hold their gathering. A man would say that they were deathless and unageing if he should then come upon the Ionians so met together. For he would see the graces of them all

Does this suggest, perhaps, some relation to Shakespeare's pastoral in Bohemia?

In any case, in Shakespeare's play the Greek decorum comes to a climax in the reading of the oracle, when many of these names converge:

OFF: You here shall swear upon this sword of justice,
      That you, Cleomenes and Dion, have

> Been both at Delphos, and from thence have
> brought
> This seal'd up Oracle, by the hand deliver'd
> Of great Apollo's priest; and that since then
> You have not dared to break the holy seal,
> Nor read the secrets in 't.

CLEO: *Dion.*   All this we swear.

LEON: Break up the seals and read.

OFF: Hermione is chaste; Polixenes blameless; Camillo
a true subject; Leontes a jealous tyrant; his innocent babe truly begotten; and the king shall live
without an heir, if that which is lost be not found.

LORDS: Now blessed be the great Apollo!

HER: Praised!

LEON: Hast thou read truth?

OFF: Ay, my lord, even so
As it is here set down.

LEON: There is no truth at all i' th' Oracle:
The sessions shall proceed: this is mere falsehood.

>   (3.2.124–41)

Leontes has committed blasphemy against the god, a point that Shakespeare has added to the story, for in Greene's romance Pandosto at once admits his folly, in an utterly limp scene, almost totally lacking in Greek atmosphere:

> Bellaria had no sooner said but the king commanded that one of his dukes should read the contents of the scroll, which after the commons had heard they gave a great shout, rejoicing and clapping their hands that the queen was clear of that false accusation. But the king, whose conscience was a witness against him of his witless fury and false suspected jealousy, was so ashamed of his rash folly that he entreated his nobles to persuade Bellaria to forgive and forget these injuries; promising not only to shew himself a loyal and loving husband, but also to reconcile himself to Egistus and Franion; revealing then before them all the cause of their secret flight, and how treacherously he thought to have practised death, if the good mind of his cupbearer had not prevented his purpose. As thus he was relating the whole matter, there was

word brought him that his young son Garinter was suddenly dead, which news so soon as Bellaria heard, sur-
charged before with extreme joy and now suppressed
with heavy sorrow, her vital spirits were so stopped that
she fell down presently dead, and could be never revived.

And she is really dead. Her restoration is all Shakespeare's work. In
this way the death of Mamillius becomes the punishment for blasphemy, as Leontes admits: "Apollo's angry, and the heavens themselves / Do strike at my injustice." And more than this. Leontes
goes on to admit that he has committed all three of the chief crimes
against the Greek conception of piety, those crimes for which the
Furies punished men: blasphemy against the gods has been preceded
by crime against a guest, the attempt to kill Polixenes, and this has
been followed by crimes against the family, the attempts to kill his
wife and his daughter. All this we realize when Leontes cries,
"Apollo, pardon / My great profaneness 'gainst thine Oracle!" and
goes on to repent of the "bloody thoughts" that he has practised
against his "kingly guest." The "piety" of Camillo, he says, "does
my deeds make the blacker!"

Such crimes form the essence of Greek tragedy. Is it then a
fantasy, or an irrelevant association, if one should be led by all these
Grecian effects to recall that Sicily was also a place which Aeschylus
visited several times, a place where he produced at least two of his
tragedies? Aeschylus died in Gela, Sicily, leaving behind the famous
epitaph thought to have been written by himself and known to
every humanist of the Renaissance:

Under this monument lies Aeschylus the Athenian,
    Euphorion's son, who died in the wheatlands of Gela. The
    grove
of Marathon with its glories can speak of his valor in battle.
The long-haired Persian remembers and can speak of it too.

Only Aeschylus himself, it seems, would have neglected to speak of
his own dramatic achievements. The association of Aeschylus with
Sicily was strengthened in the Renaissance by the tradition that he
left Athens for Sicily because he had been defeated by Simonides in
a competition for the elegy on those killed at Marathon, or, in
another tradition, because Sophocles had beaten him in a contest of
tragedies. Whatever the truth may be, these traditions firmly at-

tached Aeschylus to the Sicilian soil, so that a Renaissance man might well think of Sicily as one of the ancient homes of tragic drama. Most of this was known to anyone who could read Latin or even talk to someone who could read Latin, for this information is contained in short biographies prefixed to Renaissance editions of Aeschylus. The Latin translation of Aeschylus by Sanravius, published at Basle in 1555, is exactly the sort of edition that Shakespeare might well have read, with the quite considerable Latin that he must have learned at the Stratford Grammar School. Or perhaps Ben Johnson told him all about it.

If the Greek setting in Sicily evokes the spirit of Greek tragedy, one might go on to consider the much debated jealousy of Leontes after the manner suggested by Tillyard. "Leontes' obsession of jealousy," says Tillyard, "is terrifying in its intensity. It reminds us not of other Shakespearean tragic errors, but rather of the god-sent lunacies of Greek drama, the lunacies of Ajax and Heracles." Or, one might add, the terrible fury of the jealous Medea. From this standpoint one might develop an approach that Tillyard does not make, for he goes on to say that the jealousy is "scantily motivated" and that "indeed, it is as much a surprise to the characters in the play as it is to the reader." But if we are reading the play in the mode of Greek tragedy, we know the story already, as indeed Shakespeare's audience might have known at least the outlines of the story, when we consider the popularity of Greene's *Pandosto* and of other stories of this type.

Such an approach might solve the problem that many readers have found in what they regard as the sudden onset of Leontes' jealousy. It is possible to interpret the opening of the play so as to indicate that Leontes' jealousy is of long standing (as it is in Greene's romance), and that what we see is the final, uncontrollable outburst of a long-gathering disease—a sort of festering, incipient madness. Certainly such an interpretation can be validly and effectively presented on the stage, as the director has done in one production that I have seen, in the summer of 1975 at Stratford-on-the-Housatonic. Every word that Leontes speaks before his outburst can be spoken in a manner of taut, extreme nervous tension. And then, with increasing signs of unease, Leontes can listen to the long and very affectionate conversation between Polixenes and Hermione, and near the end can hear her say:

> Of this make no conclusion, lest you say
> Your queen and I are devils. Yet go on;
> Th' offences we have made you do, we'll answer,
> If you first sinn'd with us, and that with us
> You did continue fault, and that you slipp'd not
> With any but with us.
>
> (1.2.81–86)

At this point Leontes breaks in with his abrupt question, for which Polixenes has given the answer thirty lines before: "Is he won yet?" When Hermione says, "He'll stay, my lord," Leontes answers with the pointed remark, "At my request he would not" and then adds, "Hermione, my dearest, thou never spok'st / To better purpose." Is this equivalent to saying that she has at last made clear her guilt? Then she flies off into a heady set of questions to which Leontes seems unable to give the answer:

> What! have I twice said well? when was't before?
> I prithee tell me: cram's with praise, and make's
> As fat as tame things: one good deed, dying tongueless,
> Slaughters a thousand, waiting upon that.
> Our praises are our wages. You may ride 's
> With one soft kiss a thousand furlongs ere
> With spur we heat an acre.
>
> (1.2.90–96)

These are indeed hot words for a jealous man to hear, yet she goes on:

> But to th' goal:
> My last good deed was to entreat his stay:
> What was my first? It has an elder sister,
> Or I mistake you: O, would her name were Grace!
> But once before I spoke to th' purpose? when?
> Nay, let me have't: I long!
>
> (1.2.96–101)

But the more she gaily prods him, the less Leontes seems able to speak: he appears choked with passion, as the hidden undercurrent of his thought at last breaks forth to the audience and to himself:

> Too hot, too hot!
> To mingle friendship far, is mingling bloods.
> I have *tremor cordis* on me: my heart dances,
> But not for joy—not joy.
>
> (1.2.108–11)

I would argue, then, that there is everything in the text to warrant the assumption that Leontes has been in the grip of jealousy before the play has opened, and that the play is best presented when he is shown to be so gripped by this disease, the madness that he rightly calls *tremor cordis*. A shaking of the heart is indeed his trouble, destroying his deepest affections and turning all to hate, as with Clytemnestra or Medea.

Assuming, then, that we know the tale, we may find a Greek dramatic irony even in the bland opening speeches of courtly compliment, as Archidamus says: "If you shall chance, Camillo, to visit Bohemia, on the like occasion whereon my services are now on foot, you shall see, as I have said, great difference betwixt our Bohemia and your Sicilia" (1.1.1–4). He is of course speaking of the countries, but in the following lines the meaning shifts to apply to the two kings: "Sicilia cannot show himself over-kind to Bohemia. They were trained together in their childhoods, and there rooted betwixt them such an affection which cannot choose but branch now" (1.1.24). But the word "branch" is ambiguous: it may simply mean "grow" or it may mean "grow apart."

Likewise, the opening of the next scene presents a speech by Polixenes that may have ominous undertones:

> Nine changes of the watery star hath been
> The shepherd's note since we have left our throne
> Without a burden. Time as long again
> Would be fill'd up, my brother, with our thanks;
> And yet we should, for perpetuity,
> Go hence in debt: and therefore, like a cipher
> (Yet standing in rich place) I multiply
> With one "We thank you" many thousands moe
> That go before it.
>
> (1.2.1–8)

With the obviously pregnant Hermione standing before us, we can guess the impact this might have upon the jealous Leontes, for

Hermione bears a nine-months' *burden*—"that which is borne in the womb" (*OED*). And there are innuendoes that a jealous man might find in the words "fill'd up," "standing in rich place," and "multiply." No wonder then that Leontes' first speech may well be spoken in a dry and abrupt manner: "Stay your thanks a while / And pay them when you part" (1.2.9–10). His following speeches may be spoken in a similar tone of constraint and taciturnity. I submit that the full impact of this opening is lost if we do not assume that Leontes is already, like a Greek protagonist, in the grip of a furious jealousy, as in the *Agamemnon*, despite her protestations of love and her flattery, Clytemnestra bears in her heart a murderous hatred and a murderous plan, as everyone in the audience knew. Shakespeare too is telling an "old tale," as the title and the text itself near the close (three times) remind us.

We may then read the play as an ancient legend dealing with the problem that Polixenes sets forth near the beginning:

> We were as twinn'd lambs that did frisk i' th' sun,
> And bleat the one at th' other: what we chang'd
> Was innocence for innocence: we knew not
> The doctrine of ill-doing, nor dream'd
> That any did. Had we pursu'd that life,
> And our weak spirits ne'er been higher rear'd
> With stronger blood, we should have answer'd heaven
> Boldly "not guilty," the imposition clear'd
> Hereditary ours.
>
> (1.2.67–74)

Shakespeare, in keeping with his Greek decorum, avoids the phrase "original sin," and speaks instead of "the doctrine of ill-doing," and "the imposition . . . Hereditary ours." These are phrases that might describe the curse of the house of Atreus, the sort of hereditary curse that lies behind so much Greek tragedy. (Can we forget that Hermione, in Greek tradition, was the daughter of Menelaus and Helen and the wife of Orestes? And that in Euripides' *Andromache* she is the desperate, unhappy wife of Neoptolemus, caught in a marital tangle, before going off with Orestes?) Though Hermione goes on to speak of "devils" and "grace," the Christian implications are so muted that they do not invade the Greek decorum. Similarly the words of Polixenes a little later refer to Judas in a veiled and guarded way: "my name / Be yoked with his that did betray the Best." The rhythm would lend itself to the phrase, "Be yoked with his that did betray our Lord," but Shakespeare chooses a term that might be suited to Greek religion and philosophy. Indeed throughout this entire first action in Sicily (acts 1, 2, and 3.1.2.) there is, I believe, only one overt anachronism: Hermione's line, "The Emperor of Russia was my father." But the ancient Greeks were involved in the manufacture of Scythian gold, and Russia in any case is a close neighbour to Greece.

This first action in Sicily, then, may be said to form a Greek tragedy, like the *Agamemnon*. But the *Agamemnon* is only the first part of that trilogy in which the hereditary imposition derived from ill-doing is redeemed by a doctrine of forgiveness and by the establishment of a court of justice at the word of Athene, under the auspices of Apollo. Orestes, in the third play of that trilogy, is lying at the foot of the great statue of Athene in Athens. Then the goddess herself enters, a living presence, to redeem Orestes from his hereditary curse. Should we add this reminiscence to the other allusions to Greek tragedy and myth that have long been felt in the statue-scene of *The Winter's Tale*—the reminiscence of the *Alcestis* and the story of Pygmalion? I think we might if we could be persuaded to regard *The Winter's Tale* as a trilogy, a sort of *Leonteia*—a trilogy of redemption on the Aeschylean model, in which, as the middle part, Shakespeare has daringly chosen to present a lyric festival celebrating the powers of "great creating nature."

I am not prepared to press this idea very hard: but it may turn out to be a useful analogy that will guide us toward the play's essential design. At the very least, such an analogy may help to counteract a current tendency to see *The Winter's Tale* as a play in two parts, whereas it seems to me essential to see the play as a three-part action performed in three different literary modes: part 1, tragedy; part 2, pastoral; part 3, miracle.

Part 2 of this "trilogy" does not, I think, begin with the entry of Time the Chorus, which the folio marks as the opening of act 4—often regarded as the opening of the second part of the play conceived as a "diptych." But these act and scene divisions may have no Shakespearean authority. Let us ignore them for a time in order to explore the possibility that the second part (or second play) begins with the change of scene from Sicilia to Bohemia (3.3). It may be wrong to present the opening scenes in Bohemia as they are usually performed, without any intermission, immediately after the

tragic departure of Leontes from the stage: "Come, and lead me /
To these sorrows." A decent interval might be allowed here, to
permit the tragic possibilities to linger in the mind. Then, after the
interval, the second play (or second part) might begin—on the
seacoast of Bohemia—wherever that might be!

But what can one make, then, of the three scenes—really four
short episodes—that precede the entrance of Autolycus (at 4.3) and
the beginning of the central pastoral action? These episodes may all
be regarded as prologues or preludes, all serving together to shift
the place, the time, and the mood: the long speech of Antigonus,
recounting his dream of Hermione, is a far better formal prologue
to the new action than the familiar, almost jocular, couplets of old
father Time. The episodes work by a rapid shifting through four
different modes of speech: blank verse in the conversation between
Antigonus and the Mariner and in the soliloquy of Antigonus; low,
comical prose as Shepherd and Clown converse; familiar speech in
loose couplets from old Time; and courtly prose in the conversation
between Polixenes and Camillo. These shifting modes of speech,
breaking the tragic decorum, accord with the shifting of place,
time, and mood and prepare us to receive a new dramatic mode,
another genre from antiquity—but here blended with modern English elements to form a timeless pastoral. We have moved into a
never-never land, a world that is at once primitive and idyllic, a
world where the sinking of a ship with all hands and the rending of
a body by a bear may be turned to comedy. It is, above all, a world
where the doctrine of ill-doing and the imposition hereditary ours
can be suspended, a world where "things dying" can be removed
from sight, so that "things new-born" can be allowed to flourish.
The central action then begins with the entrance of Autolycus,
singing a song of nature's renewal:

> When daffodils begin to peer,
>   With heigh! the doxy over the dale,
> Why then comes in the sweet o' the year,
>   For the red blood reigns in the winter's pale.
>
> The lark, that tirra-lirra chants,
>   With heigh! with heigh! the thrush and the jay,
> Are summer songs for me and my aunts,
>   While we lie tumbling in the hay.
>
>   (4.3.1–4, 9–12)

Then he identifies himself: "My father named me Autolycus; who, being as I am, littered under Mercury, was likewise a snapper-up of unconsidered trifles" (4.3.24–26). Autolycus was the name of the grandfather of the wily Odysseus; the son of the god Hermes by Chione, in an incident closely related to Apollo and Delphi in Ovid's version of the tale:

> Daedalion had a daughter, Chione, a girl of fourteen who, being ripe for marriage and endowed with rare beauty, had a thousand suitors. Now Phoebus and Maia's son, Mercury, chanced to be returning, the one from his beloved Delphi, and the other from the summit of Cyllene. They both saw the girl at the same moment and both, at the same moment, fell in love. Apollo deferred his hopes of enjoying her love till night-time, but Mercury, impatient of delay, touched the girl's face with his rod that brings slumber. At that potent touch, she lay still, and suffered the god's violent embrace. Then, when night had scattered the heavens with stars, Phoebus, disguised as an old woman, enjoyed the pleasure which another had had before him. In the fullness of time, Chione bore twins: to the wing-footed god an artful child, Autolycus, who was up to all manner of tricks, accustomed to turn black to white and white to black, a true son of his crafty father, and to Phoebus, a son Philammon, renowned for his singing and his playing of the lyre.

Shakespeare's Autolycus appears to be a blending of the qualities of this twin birth, his thievery being derived from Hermes, his gift of song from Apollo.

The allusion is important to this second part, for Autolycus serves as a benevolent presence over the whole festival scene, enriching it (and himself) with his tricks and ballads. I say a beneficent presence, for along with his petty thievery he brings joy and song to the shepherd's feast. He sells them what they want, and his cutting of purses while they are entranced with singing his ballads seems rather an appropriate reward for the pleasure that he has brought to them. He prances throughout this second part like a good-humoured satyr; his amorality is harmless, and his singing, if well-performed, could suggest powers beyond his beggarly tatters.

In spite of his roguery he brings health, sanity, play, and happiness
to the scene. Furthermore, he concludes the second part of the
"trilogy" with services of aid to the escape of the young couple,
providing (perforce) the garments of disguise; he knows all, he
overhears all, and thus he helps the prince by being true, as he says,
to his own principles of knavery, when he deflects the shepherds,
father and son, from going to the King with their story. He
dominates the last 250 lines of the second part with his ingenious
and voluble prose. What the shepherds say at the close turns out to
be true:

> CLO: We are blest in this man, as I may say, even blest.
> SHEP: Let's before, as he bids us: he was provided to do
>   us good.
>
> (4.4.829–30)

Thus Autolycus presides over the Bohemian scene, concluding
with aid and hope, just as he has brought at his entrance the
summer songs that dominate the festival. Summer songs: it is
essential to get the season right, for there has been some puzzlement
about it, because of a misunderstanding of Perdita's account of
autumnal flowers. Perdita first takes Polixenes and Camillo at the
surface level of their disguise, as old men with grey beards, and
welcomes them accordingly:

> Reverend sirs,
> For you, there's rosemary, and rue; these keep
> Seeming and savour all the winter long:
> Grace and remembrance be to you both,
> And welcome to our shearing!
>
> (4.4.73–77)

Polixenes then answers, saying,

> Shepherdess—
> A fair one are you—well you fit our ages
> With flowers of winter.
>
> (4.4.77–79)

Perdita then apologizes by saying that she has to give herbs of
winter because she has no autumnal flowers available, and she
explains why this is so:

> Sir, the year growing ancient,
> Not yet on summer's death nor on the birth
> Of trembling winter, the fairest flowers o' th' season
> Are our carnations and streak'd gillyvors,
> Which some call nature's bastards: of that kind
> Our rustic garden's barren; and I care not
> To get slips of them.
>
> (4.4.79–85)

She is not saying that the year is "growing ancient" at this moment. She is saying that these flowers which, because of their hardiness, last far on into the autumn, might be growing now, but she has chosen not to plant them, and therefore she has none of them to give. As she goes on to converse with Polixenes she appears to sense from his talking that he is much younger than his disguise indicates and so she offers them midsummer flowers:

> Here's flowers for you:
> Hot lavender, mints, savory, marjoram,
> The marigold, that goes to bed wi' th' sun
> And with him rises, weeping: these are flowers
> Of middle summer, and I think they are given
> To men of middle age. Y'are very welcome.
>
> (4.4.103–8)

Midsummer Day, June 24, was a time of ancient festival (coming at about the time of sheep-shearing)—the "Midsummer Ale," it was called, just as the Whitsuntide festival was known as the "Whitsun Ale" (the celebration that Perdita mentions a little later as "Whitsun pastorals" bedecked with flowers). Shakespeare is here recalling three great English summer festivals of fertility: the sheep-shearing, the Midsummer Day, the Whitsun Ale. In this context little Christian connotation can remain in the word Whitsun, and there is no exclusively Christian connotation in the old shepherd's fear that he will have "no priest" to "shovel in dust" on his corpse. Fear of lying unburied was a deep aspect of Greek religious feeling, as the *Antigone* demonstrates.

Then, as Perdita turns to "Doricles," Shakespeare creates his delicate blending of English flowers and Grecian myths:

> O Proserpina,
> For the flowers now that, frighted, thou let'st fall
> From Dis's waggon! daffodils,

> That come before the swallow dares, and take
> The winds of March with beauty; violets, dim,
> But sweeter than the lids of Juno's eyes
> Or Cytherea's breath; pale primroses,
> That die unmarried, ere they can behold
> Bright Phoebus in his strength.
>
> (4.4.116–24)

The mention of Phoebus takes us back to the opening of this scene, where the prince uses the Greek myths of metamorphosis to tell Perdita that it is quite proper for her to be attired in a manner that suggests the goddess Flora, and for him to be disguised as the shepherd Doricles:

> The gods themselves,
> Humbling their deities to love, have taken
> The shapes of beasts upon them: Jupiter
> Became a bull, and bellow'd; the green Neptune
> A ram, and bleated; and the fire-rob'd god,
> Golden Apollo, a poor humble swain,
> As I seem now.
>
> (4.4.25–31)

Thus Greek mythology blends with English country ways and wares, and so, instead of a morris dance, the festival concludes when "three carters, three shepherds, three neat-herds, and three swine-herds" make themselves "all men of hair" and present a dance of twelve satyrs. It is a suitable finale for a world without time or place—just before that world is shattered by the re-emergence of the tragic element, as the King unmasks.

Another intermission is desirable before the third part of the "trilogy" begins with a return to the Sicilian scene, where a strong new note emerges in the opening lines, as Cleomenes says to Leontes:

> Sir, you have done enough, and have perform'd
> A *saint-like* sorrow: no *fault* could you make,
> Which you have not *redeem'd*; indeed, paid down
> More *penitence* than done *trespass*: at the last,
> Do as the heavens have done, forget your *evil*;
> With them, *forgive* yourself.
>
> (5.1.1–6)

I have italicized the words that set the theme, words that provide a much stronger tinge of Christian reference than anything found earlier in the play. They begin to shift the balance away from things Greek or pagan toward things Christian, things contemporary with Shakespeare. Apollo still is mentioned, but now we begin to feel some special reason for that Christian name, Paulina. She is a bitter reminder of the evil that Leontes has done; she is his conscience, and her words lead toward a scene that may be called a restoration by faith. I cannot, however, agree with those who would attempt to make the whole "trilogy" into a fable of Christian fall and salvation. *The Winter's Tale* moves from ancient Greek, to timeless pagan, to something very close to contemporary Christian. The triumph of time runs through the ages of human history, not only in one family. Now, in part 3, the language throughout becomes more explicitly Christian. Hermione is spoken of as a "sainted spirit" and the servant, praising Perdita's beauty, asserts, in strongly contemporary terms,

> This is a creature,
> Would she begin a *sect*, might quench the *zeal*
> Of all *professors* else; make *proselytes*
> Of who she but bid follow.
> (5.1.106–9)

In this context the word "professors" is bound to recall such sixteenth-century phrases as "professors of Christ's name and doctrine," or "the professors of God's truth in England."

More and more, within the classical colouring, the Christian note seems struggling to be born, as when Leontes cries out to Florizel:

> The *blessed* gods
> Purge all infection from our air whilst you
> Do climate here! You have a *holy father*,
> A *graceful* gentleman; against whose person
> (So *sacred* as it is) I have done *sin*,
> For which, the heavens (taking angry note)
> Have left me issueless: and your father's *blest*
> (As he from *heaven* merits it) with you,
> Worthy his *goodness*.
> (5.1.167–75)

The plural "gods" and plural "heavens" become in the parenthesis a singular "heaven."

Then in the penultimate scene, although the recognition of Perdita offstage is narrated after the fashion of a Greek messenger, the effect nevertheless becomes contemporary with 1611, as Autolycus hears the three anonymous gentlemen narrate in courtly prose the miracle of this recovery: "they looked as they had heard of a world ransomed, or one destroyed." Bonfires have been lit, ballad-makers cannot express the wonder, and best of all, we have word now of Hermione's statue: "a piece many years in doing and now newly performed by that rare Italian master, Julio Romano" (5.2.94–95). Here at last, with this allusion to the art of Raphael's partner, we have the one great undeniable anachronism in Sicilia, but it is carefully placed, carefully designed, to bring us fully into the world of Shakespeare's humanism. Appropriately, the director of the 1975 production in Connecticut placed Hermione as statue in the garb and posture of a Renaissance madonna. The effect was breathtaking, and properly foreshadowed the restoration soon to be revealed, as Paulina says first to Leontes, "It is requir'd / You do awake your faith," and then says to Hermione:

> 'Tis time; descend; be stone no more; approach;
> Strike all that look upon with marvel. Come!
> I'll fill your grave up: stir, nay, come away:
> Bequeath to death your numbness; for from him
> Dear life redeems you.
>
> (5.3.99–103)

We have moved from the ancient tragedy of blood through the cyclical, pagan world of great creating nature, and on now to the present time when, in humanist terms, faith, nourished by art and grace, may witness a triumphant restoration of the world to goodness. Yet Mamillius and Antigonus are dead, and Hermione's wrinkles remain, the finest touch of Shakespeare's realism.

Shakespeare's Bohemia Revisited: A Caveat

Richard Studing

In approaching the pastoral scene in *The Winter's Tale* as an idyll and place of relief from the falseness and misery of courtly life, commentators have dwelled, generally and specifically, on the simplicity, naturalness, and pristine values of Bohemia. The entire country scene, with its trappings of shepherds and shepherdesses, sheep-shearing festival, dances, rustic foolery, and rustic lovemaking, has often been idealized as an Arcadia, an Eden of love, friendship, and good will. Edwin Greenlaw considers it to be "the most exquisite and satisfying pastoral in Elizabethan literature." Much in the same spirit, G. Wilson Knight believes the Pastoral Scene "sums up and surpasses all Shakespeare's earlier poetry of pastoral and romance."

More specifically, much consideration has been given to the simple nobility and virtue of country life, which are thought to outshine vigorously the woe and destruction bred in Sicilia's court. The natural piety and conduct of the old Shepherd and his son, for instance, have been singled out as somewhat naïve but nevertheless virtuous *exempla* eclipsing the uncharitable deeds committed by King Leontes. Perdita has been frequently cited as the most profound symbol and promise of rebirth in the pastoral world. She is looked upon as a fertility goddess who, along with the movements of nature, will bring the spring of new life out of the wintry barrenness ushered in by Leontes' passion. Perdita's frank, innocent

From *Shakespeare Studies: An Annual Gathering of Research, Criticism and Reviews* 15. © 1982 by the Council for Research in the Renaissance.

relationship with Florizel, contrasted with the sinfully infected love of her parents, is viewed as further assurance that her symbolic role will be fulfilled spontaneously and naturally. Moreover, because of her noble birth and country nurture, Perdita is thought of as the natural bond between Sicilia and Bohemia. Therefore, she is seen as an integral part of the court-country theme, symbolizing the union of the two kingdoms. Florizel, too, is said to take on mythic qualities that complement Perdita's symbolic stature. He is associated with the folklore figure of the lover prince who possesses the innate ability to recognize immediately the real character of his rustic queen. And he is, in the words of S. L. Bethell, prepared "to sacrifice royalty for love."

However, this highly idealized approach praising the prettiness, congeniality, and morality of Shakespeare's pastoral is only one side of the story. And, in actuality, not a very strong side at that. It is true, as Philip M. Weinstein suggested, that in this scene Shakespeare has departed far from pastoral conventions and that the realism of the scene exposes the inadequacy of the idealism it attempts to convey. But what of pastoral convention and realism in *The Winter's Tale*—how do they work? I suggest that the pastoral mode is really used not as convention but, rather, as a vehicle to develop and forward the story. It is convention only in that it serves as a traditional scenic contrast to life at court. Act 4, scene 4, can be viewed as *antipastoral* in that the pastoral tradition (including realism) is subordinated to and submerged in dramatic exigency. Instead of pastoral convention or conventions, we have pastoral *devices* that function to mirror courtly values and echo Leontes' sinful passion. Especially in context of the first three acts of the play, the situations of pastoralism often cast a negative aura on country life.

In the structure of *The Winter's Tale*, no one and no place are exempt from the passion of "that fatal country Sicilia." In Bohemia, Polixenes is overcome by an egocentric, tyrannic passion akin to Leontes'. Perdita endures a fate similar to Queen Hermione's when Polixenes learns of her relationship with Florizel, and like the Queen, she is forced to flee royal wrath. Florizel's departure from paternal tyranny parallels the death of Mamillius who, unlike his counterpart, did not possess the years nor the strength to survive his overwhelmingly tragic environment. The shepherds, too, by succumbing to the riches of court are victims of Sicilia's corruption.

These and other "pastoral" echoes and reflections of courtly life cannot be ignored. The general pastoral formula of posing a serious "value-contrast" between the pastoral world and another kind of society does not work out satisfactorily in the drama. The objective of my essay is to examine the pastoral scenes of the play in light of their dramatic value, with particular reference to structure and theme, and to show, as Harold Jenkins says of *As You Like It*, that "In city or country, *all* ways of life are at bottom the same."

The immediate connection between Leontes and the Bohemian countryside occurs in the first time sequence of the play with the appearance of the Shepherd in act 3, scene 3, just after Antigonus has exposed the infant Perdita to the elements and he is pursued and destroyed by the bear. The Shepherd's opening lines (ll. 59–67) before discovering Perdita are revealing:

> I would there were no age between ten and three-and-twenty, or that youth would sleep out the rest; for there is nothing in the between but getting wenches with child, wronging the ancientry, stealing, fighting—Hark you now! Would any but these boiled-brains of nineteen and two-and-twenty hunt this weather? They have scared away two of my best sheep, which I fear the wolf will sooner find than the master.

Suggestively, the references to "youth," "getting wenches with child," "stealing," and "fighting" point to the complexities of the Leontes–Polixenes conflict. In this context, "wronging the an-cientry" recalls Leontes' violation of kingship by his tyrannic impositions on his aged counselor, Camillo, and, for that matter, the entire court. Even the plight of the Shepherd's two best sheep, who have been scared away and are now lost and liable prey for the wolf, brings to mind Leontes' treatment of Mamillius and Perdita; at the same time, it forecasts the oncoming danger of Florizel and Perdita at the hands of Polixenes. When the Shepherd finds the deserted infant, he gives an accurate appraisal of the situation: "This has been some stair-work, some trunk-work, some behind-door work" (3.3.73–75). The Shepherd's remarks are reflective of past action: the jealous suspicions of Leontes; his devious plot for revenge; the escape of Polixenes and Camillo; the abandonment of Perdita; and retrospectively, they suggest Paulina's grand clandestine plan of Hermione's concealment. In a contracted statement, the

Shepherd has recapitulated, by indirection, the core of events of the first three acts. But the emphatic warning of the antipastoralism of the Bohemian setting comes when the Shepherd, joined by the Clown, discovers the "bearing-cloth" accompanying the infant. Here we learn that rural Bohemia is a fallen world, "a world of corruption" that will live "out an immense fraud." The optimistic and humanitarian aspect of the discovery of the foundling, which is often referred to, is clouded by an excessive concern with "fairy gold": "look thee here; take up, take up, boy; open't. So, let's see: it was told me I should be rich by the fairies" (3.3.115–16). Furthermore, the Shepherd discards his lost sheep, the staple and symbol of pastoral life, in favor of rushing off to the cottage with the riches of court: "Let my sheep go: come, good boy, the next way home" (3.3.124–25). From this point on, the corrupted pastoral becomes a dominant theme in act 4.

Like act 3, scene 2, the first two scenes of the fourth act are transitional; although act 4, scene 1, is a bridge and introduction to the pastoral world in the drama's new time sequence and act 4, scene 2, actually begins that sequence. The awkwardly structured first scene does, in its own way, look forward to new action, and it reflects on activities during the sixteen-year time lapse as well. In his cryptic manner, Time says that he tries "all" with "both joy and terror / Of good and bad, that makes and unfolds error" (4.1.1–2). Time has already tried Leontes, the breeder of error, and in consequence the innocent Mamillius has been taken by the scythe of death. Right at the moment of Time's appearance, both Leontes and Hermione are suffering in reclusive existence, deprived of the fruits of marriage. Also, Time's speech can be directed at Bohemia: the country swains who get "wenches with child," the shepherds enthralled by wealth, and the future tyrannic outbursts of Polixenes, for example. Of course, Time does, by spanning "that wide gap," fulfill his obligation by telling us of Leontes' penitential seclusion, bringing us to "fair Bohemia," and informing us of the status and maturity of Perdita.

Besides placing us in the new time sequence in Bohemia, act 4, scene 2, it has an expository function. And, concomitantly, the scene echoes some of the themes we have previously encountered, giving dramatic coherence to the play in spite of the time gap. As exposition, both Polixenes and Camillo declare, and certainly with much emphasis, that Florizel (recalling Prince Hal) is delinquent from his filial and princely obligations and that he is involved with "a most homely shepherd" who has "a daughter of most rare note" (4.2.39, 42–43); this naturally introduces the Florizel–Perdita episodes to come. Dramatically, the delinquency of Florizel is a restatement of the theme of separation between parent and offspring. On the level of romance, Florizel's absence and involvement in "happier affairs" are neatly explained by his mythic role of the lover prince who pursues the disguised princess, wins her, flees with her from parental opposition, and after much complication attains felicity. However, this explanation oversimplifies and perhaps confuses the more complex structure of the play. For Polixenes must, out of dramatic necessity, enact the part of tyrant in order to generate the drama to resolution in Sicilia. As shown in the sheepshearing scene, Polixenes' attack on Florizel and Perdita is closer to the tyranny of Leontes than the conventional *senex* figure of New Comedy. Thus, the restatement of the separation theme in Florizel's absence from court should be considered in the same light as the Leontes–Mamillius and Leontes–Perdita relationships. Finally, act 4, scene 2, emphasizes rustic wealth. We are informed that the Shepherd has assumed courtly values and risen to high estate in rural Bohemia. Polixenes himself is astonished when he speaks of a "man, they say, that from very nothing, and beyond the imagination of his neighbours, is grown into an unspeakable estate" (4.3.39–41). Structurally, the ornamented rusticity of the Shepherd's cottage becomes the focal point of the main action and complication of act 4, and therefore attracts and gathers the principal characters for movement back to Sicilia and denouement of the play at Leontes' court.

Critics have considered act 4, scene 3, a bridge to the sheepshearing festival and observed that, by means of farce, this scene affords the playwright an opportunity to introduce Autolycus into his dramatic scheme. Aside from its excellent farce, the scene, because of its comic sophistication, becomes an ironic commentary on the characters and situations in the play. Indeed, when Autolycus enters the rustic world, he dupes and even robs the gullible Clown in what has been said to be a parody of the Good Samaritan Parable; but Autolycus does not enter a world of innocence. In view of his hilarious comic spirit and genial corruption, the rogue has been associated with Falstaff and called the Lord of Misrule of *The Winter's Tale*. Virtually, misrule has governed the drama long before his arrival. It might be said that Autolycus, like the old Shepherd, is a realist who, as best he can and in the only way he can, takes advantage of what opportunity offers him.

Autolycus's opening lines, including his two songs, establish him as a linking character between court and country. From the bits of information concerning his history, we see that he is another embodiment of courtly sophistication and corruption invading the Bohemian countryside; this time the corruption comes from the quarter of Polixenes' court. We hear, for instance, that Autolycus is an ex-courtier who has fallen from court favor and degenerated to the ranks of thievery and roguery. Now, he tells us, he is "out of service" (4.3.14) and has been "whipped out of court" (4.3.87)—undoubtedly because of vice. The most startling thing is that he was in the service of Florizel, and we wonder if the prince ousted the rogue. This, of course, relates Autolycus to Polixenes and Camillo and even the infant Perdita, all of whom have been, so to speak, whipped out of the Sicilian court by Leontes. Surely, Florizel can be added to this consort when he leaves his father's court for the refreshing affairs of the country. Very clearly, Bohemia and its rural regions have become a haven for exiles and outcasts.

The comic encounter of Autolycus and the Clown at lines 32–120 obviously prepares us for the climax of act 4 at the country festival. More than this, it brings to the foreground a variation on the theme of rustic wealth. On his appearance, the Clown is engrossed and preoccupied with an extraordinary list of items which Perdita desires for the celebration: sugar, "five pound of currants, rice . . . saffron to colour the warden pies," and spices. To augment this fantastic list, an extravagant musical entertainment is planned. The Clown, not as dull-witted as we might imagine, is quick to remark that his sister "lays it on" (4.3.40). This excessive, if not ostentatious, show of finery tightens the bond between court and country even more.

Act 4, scene 4, with its festive splendor and colorful spectacle, comes closer to courtly grandeur and extravagance than to the rustic simplicity of a rural feast. The elaborate preparations, dances, songs, and performers, three of whom, we are told, "hath danced before the king" (4.4.337–38), indeed, give the impression that rusticity has been overwhelmed by aristocratic artifice. In fact, the natural world has been so converted that Florizel succumbs to its seductiveness by calling it "a meeting of the petty gods." The artificiality of the sheep-shearing scene is extended to the characters who, like performers in a play within a play, act out their roles in disguises and false identities. Perdita is the glorious queen allied with Flora, "Most goddess-like prank'd up," and Florizel is her lowly swain. Polixenes and Camillo, too, play their parts as disguised mock visitors. As the prince states, the gods have undergone a metamorphosis: they "have taken / The shapes of beasts upon them" (4.4.26–27). Autolycus's singing entrance with his pack of disguises and cosmetics is a comic remark on the whole situation. Later, Autolycus and Florizel switch costumes, and the old Shepherd and Clown are transmuted into courtiers in the final act.

The conscious artifice of the festival and Perdita's prominent role as its queen incite us to believe that the Shepherd has designed this feast for the sake of Florizel—to impress and enchant him. For Perdita is well aware of his royal station and the Shepherd knows him. "To have a worthy feeding" (4.4.171) and offers to match Florizel's "portion" with an equal dowry for his daughter (4.4.385–87). Perdita herself displays élan and a great seductive power. Her rustic beauty not only wins the adoration of the prince, but it also charms Polixenes and Camillo. Camillo, after receiving flowers from her, says:

> I should leave grazing, were I of your flock,
> And only live by gazing.
>
> (4.4.109–10)

And Polixenes is taken with this "prettiest low-born lass" that "smacks of something greater than herself, / Too noble for this place" (4.4.156, 158–59). Florizel is intoxicated by the loveliness of Perdita, and he is caught up in the movement and sweep of festival. Although the "year [is] growing ancient" (4.4.79), the prince views his queen as "Flora / Peering in April's front" (4.4.2–3). Most certainly, she is his goddess, and for her, he, like a Proteus, transforms and humbles himself as an obscure swain.

There has been a good deal of commentary on the art-nature "debate" between Perdita and Polixenes (ll. 79–103) and its relationship to Renaissance theories of art. The center of the various critical discussions of the "debate" has been the contrast of Perdita's argument favoring the purity of nature over the false, mimetic quality of art, and Polixenes' belief that art improves nature. Moreover, it has been recognized that there is irony in Polixenes' position. In opposing the union of Florizel ("gentler scion") and Perdita ("wildest stock"), he contradicts the application of his own theory to produce a "nobler stock" by means of grafting. The irony is much deeper and dramatically organic than this, because it strikes at the heart and foundation of the fusion of court and country. Considering Polixenes' viewpoint, and he is not aware of it, the values and artifice of courtly life have already been fused or grafted with the "wildest stock" of Bohemia. Later in the scene, to cite another instance, we witness the country girls, Mopsa and Dorcas, hovering about Autolycus's wares of "Masks for faces," necklaces, and "Perfume for a lady's chamber" (4.4.223–25); the maidens are eager to embrace the sophistication of the city. When Perdita says to Polixenes:

> the fairest flowers o' th' season
> Are our carnations and streak'd gillyvors,
> Which some call nature's bastards: of that kind
> Our rustic garden's barren; and I care not
> To get slips of them
>
> (4.4.81–85)

she, as rustic goddess and queen, somewhat violates her own argument. Like the flowers she finds distasteful, Perdita is herself a misfit, who stands out radiantly and extraordinarily in her environment. Perdita realizes her behavior and attire exceed her position and expresses this self-consciously on two occasions: first to Florizel,

> Your high self,
> The gracious mark o' th' land, you have obscur'd
> With a swain's wearing, and me, poor lowly maid,
> Most goddess-like prank'd up
>
> (4.4.7–10)

and, again, after Polixenes' rage, when she will "queen it no inch farther, / But milk [her] ewes, and weep" (4.4.450–51). What she does not realize, however, is that, in her desire to consummate her love for Florizel in marriage, she is taking Polixenes' stand in the "debate"; both she and the prince are attempting to complete the grafting process suggested by Polixenes. At this point, neither lover is aware of Perdita's royal birth.

From the "debate" up to Polixenes' tyrannic destruction of the feast at lines 419–42, the pagan, festive tempo of the scene increases: music, dance, love, and sensual rhetoric are highlighted. Once again, we are reminded that the Bohemian festival has become a spectacle far beyond the compass of rural pleasure. Perdita, who has been transformed from goddess and queen to an innocent flower maiden, now assumes the role of a risqué May Queen. In an enticing rhapsody, she praises the joys of sexual fulfillment and is aggressive in her display of love to her prince. Reminiscent of the poetry of Herrick, Perdita laments the growing maidenheads of youth and the fact that she has no "flowers o' th' spring"—flowers that symbolize fertility and youthful potency—for either Florizel or the rustic maidens. And in sexual language, she recalls Juno, Cytherea, and the flowers of the early year:

> pale primroses,
> That die unmarried, ere they can behold
> Bright Phoebus in his strength (a malady
> Most incident to maids).
>
> (4.4.122–25)

Perdita's expression of love overpowers Florizel: she would "strew him o'er and o'er" with garlands and flowers "like a bank, for love to lie and play on" (4.4.129–30), and would have him "quick, and in [her] arms" (l. 132). Her direct erotic statements and Florizel's enthusiastic response:

> When you speak, sweet,
> I'd have you do it ever: when you sing,
> I'd have you buy and sell so, so give alms,
> Pray so, and, for the ord'ring your affairs,
> To sing them too: when you do dance, I wish you
> A wave o' th' sea, that you might ever do
> Nothing but that, move still, still so,
> And own no other function
>
> (4.4.136–43)

culminate in a dance of shepherds and shepherdesses, a dance of fertility symbolizing their sexual union.

Following this entertainment and the songs of Autolycus and the rustic girls, a group of carters, shepherds, neatherds, and swineherds enters disguised as "men of hair" to perform a dance of twelve satyrs. Beyond its contribution to the festive spirit of the scene, this dance, too, has significance. Traditionally, the satyr figure, with its lascivious nature and repulsive aspect, represented disruption of order and the basic struggle between the two parts of man: body and spirit. Regarding theme and motif, the appearance of the satyrs embodies and amalgamates all the overt and suggestive expressions of lust and bawdy which have appeared in the drama up to now. As we know, lust first originated as a germ in the fantasy and diseased psyche of Leontes. It was then manifested in his dream of jealousy and unfounded bawdy rhetoric, and it has appeared intermittently ever since. Perhaps it is dramatically appropriate to conjure up, in this extremely histrionic fashion, the play's motif and link the satyr figure to Leontes. In connection with the Bohemian countryside, the dance of the satyrs is further indication of the imposition of court on country. The dance itself is a property of court values and entertainment, and it is King Polixenes who, with gusto, welcomes the wild dancers: "You weary those that refresh us: pray, let's see these four threes of herdsmen" (4.4.335–36). Dramatically, the dance signals the destruction of the feast and the attempted destruction of the love of Florizel and Perdita. Immediately after the dance, Polixenes states to Camillo: "Is it not too far gone? 'Tis time to part them" (l. 345), a preface to his reenactment of Leontes' tyranny.

The tyranny of Polixenes replicates in several ways Leontes' passionate outbursts earlier in the play. Most obviously, Polixenes attempts to destroy love, and he therefore violates the natural potential of procreation. In the case of each king, the love to be destroyed is closely related to the tyrant himself. Upon unmasking himself from his disguise, Polixenes attacks Perdita in the same vindictive, hostile manner Leontes employed against Hermione. Both kings view the female as seductive and promiscuous. Leontes sees his wife as a playful "adultress," a "bed-swerver," who is big with Polixenes' child (2.1.88, 93); and Polixenes calls Perdita a "fresh piece / Of excellent witchcraft" and "enchantment," who has opened "these rural latches" to royalty (4.4.423–24, 435, 439). His bawdy language surely echoes Leontes' jealous speeches. Further, Polixenes' threats to have Perdita's "beauty scratch'd with briars and made / More homely than [her] state" (4.4.426–27) and his belligerent treatment of the old Shepherd bring to mind Leontes' terrible plans for his family and friend. At this moment of dramatic crisis in the pastoral world, Polixenes has transformed himself into a personification of the grotesque satyr figure which he had enthusiastically welcomed to the festival.

The splendor, extravagance, and dream texture of the sheep-shearing festival have been shattered. And all the characters are awakened to the reality of sin and its destructive force. The youthful dreams of love and marriage, the dreams of enlarged rustic wealth, and the "courtly illusion" of rural Bohemia are reduced to the coarseness of Polixenes' act. For salvation, the inhabitants of the green world must make flight, must "make for Sicilia," and confront the seat of original sin.

The festive beauty and dramatic energy of Shakespeare's pastoral are undeniable, and it is an appropriate prelude to the incredible statue scene in act 5. Also, there is no question that act 4, scene 4, foreshadows a regeneration and rebirth of the old Sicilian world. However, "pure symbolic rebirth" and pastoral idealism are blemished by realism; it is not so much the realism of E. M. W. Tillyard's view of country life "given the fullest force of actuality," but dramatic realism: the realism of a pastoral world which has inherited the values and fallibilities of court, a pastoral world that needs regeneration and resolution itself. For dramatic coherence, the pretenses and conflicts of Bohemia must, like Sicilia, be unmasked and resolved. These pretenses and conflicts are what John P. Cutts sees as an "immense fraud" and what Philip M. Weinstein means by Bohemia's "vivid and conflict-breeding realism (so unexpected in pastoral)." From this standpoint, act 4, scene 4, and the other country scenes counter the nature of pastoralism. Bohemia is not a refuge offering a serious value contrast to another society. In *The Winter's Tale*, the tensions of court and country must completely unwind, which occurs in the final act when Hermione "awakens." This kind of resolution is demanded by the play's structure and themes. Certainly, readers and viewers who insist upon highly idealized interpretations of the Bohemian pastoral run a risk, like the characters themselves, of being lulled into idyllic dreams.

Chronology

1564	William Shakespeare born at Stratford-on-Avon to John Shakespeare, a butcher, and Mary Arden. He is baptized on April 26.
1582	Marries Anne Hathaway in November.
1583	Daughter Susanna born, baptized on May 26.
1585	Twins Hamnet and Judith born, baptized on February 2.
1588–90	Sometime during these years, Shakespeare goes to London, without family.
1588–89	First plays are performed in London.
1590–92	*The Comedy of Errors*, the three parts of *Henry VI*.
1593–94	Publication of *Venus and Adonis* and *The Rape of Lucrece*, both dedicated to the Earl of Southampton. Shakespeare becomes a sharer in the Lord Chamberlain's company of actors. *The Taming of the Shrew*, *Two Gentlemen of Verona*, *Richard III*.
1595–97	*Romeo and Juliet*, *Richard II*, *King John*, *A Midsummer Night's Dream*, *Love's Labour's Lost*.
1596	Son Hamnet dies. Grant of arms to father.
1597	*The Merchant of Venice*, *Henry IV, Part 1*. Purchases New Place in Stratford.
1598–1600	*Henry IV, Part 2*, *As You Like It*, *Much Ado about Nothing*, *Twelfth Night*, *The Merry Wives of Windsor*, *Henry V*, and *Julius Caesar*. Moves his company to the new Globe Theatre.
1601	*Hamlet*. Shakespeare's father dies, buried on September 8.
1603	Death of Queen Elizabeth; James VI of Scotland becomes James I of England; Shakespeare's company becomes the King's Men.

1603–4	*All's Well That Ends Well, Measure for Measure, Othello*.
1605–6	*King Lear, Macbeth*.
1607	Marriage of daughter Susanna on June 5.
1607–8	*Timon of Athens, Antony and Cleopatra, Pericles*.
1608	Death of Shakespeare's mother. Buried on September 9.
1609	*Cymbeline*. Publication of sonnets. Shakespeare's company purchases Blackfriars Theatre.
1610–11	*The Winter's Tale, The Tempest*. Shakespeare retires to Stratford.
1616	Marriage of daughter Judith on February 10. William Shakespeare dies at Stratford on April 23.
1623	Publication of the Folio edition of Shakespeare's plays.

Contributors

HAROLD BLOOM, Sterling Professor of the Humanities at Yale University, is the author of *The Anxiety of Influence, Poetry and Repression,* and many other volumes of literary criticism. His forthcoming study, *Freud: Transference and Authority,* attempts a full-scale reading of all of Freud's major writings. A MacArthur Prize Fellow, he is general editor of five series of literary criticism published by Chelsea House.

G. WILSON KNIGHT was Professor of English at the University of Leeds. His many influential books include *The Wheel of Fire, The Imperial Theme, The Burning Oracle, The Mutual Flame, The Christian Renaissance, The Shakespearean Tempest, Christ and Nietzsche,* and *The Starlit Dome.*

JAMES EDWARD SIEMON has also written on *Cymbeline.*

L. C. KNIGHTS is Professor Emeritus of English at Cambridge University. Among his many works are "How Many Children Had Lady Macbeth: An Essay in Theory and Practice of Shakespeare Criticism," *An Approach to Hamlet, Some Shakespearean Themes,* and *Drama and Society in the Age of Jonson.*

CAROL THOMAS NEELY teaches in the Department of English at Illinois State University. She is the author of *Broken Nuptials in Shakespeare's Plays* and *Speaking True: Shakespeare's Use of the Elements of Pastoral Romance,* and is coeditor of *The Woman's Part,* an anthology of feminist criticism on Shakespeare.

CHARLES FREY is Professor of English at the University of Washington at Seattle. He is the author of *Shakespeare's Vast Romance: A Study of* The Winter's Tale.

ANNE BARTON is Fellow of New College and University Lecturer in English, Oxford University. She is the author of *Shakespeare and the Idea of the Play* and *Ben Jonson, Dramatist*.

LOUIS L. MARTZ, Sterling Professor Emeritus of English at Yale University, is the author of *The Poetry of Meditation, John Donne and Meditation: The Anniversaries, The Paradise Within: Studies in Vaughan, Traherne, and Milton*, and *The Poem of the Mind*.

RICHARD STUDING is Professor of Humanities at Wayne State University and coeditor of *Mannerism in Art, Literature, and Music: A Bibliography*.

Bibliography

Barber, C. L. *Shakespeare's Festive Comedy*. Princeton: Princeton University Press, 1959.

Bartholomeusz, Dennis. The Winter's Tale *in Performance in England and America: 1611–1976*. Cambridge: Cambridge University Press, 1982.

Battenhouse, R. W. "Theme and Structure in *The Winter's Tale*." *Shakespeare Survey* 33 (1980): 123–38.

Bellette, A. F. "Truth and Utterance in *The Winter's Tale*." *Shakespeare Survey* 31 (1978): 65–75.

Bethell, S. L. The Winter's Tale: *A Study*. London: Staples Press, 1947.

Bryant, J. A., Jr. "Shakespeare's Allegory: *The Winter's Tale*." *Sewanee Review* 63 (1955): 202–22.

Champion, Larry S. *The Evolution of Shakespeare's Comedy: A Study in Dramatic Perspective*. Cambridge, Mass.: Harvard University Press, 1970.

Coghill, Nevill. "Six Points of Stage-Craft in *The Winter's Tale*." *Shakespeare Survey* 11 (1958): 31–41.

Colie, Rosalie. *Shakespeare's Living Art*. Princeton: Princeton University Press, 1974.

Cox, Lee Sheridan. "The Role of Autolycus in *The Winter's Tale*." *Studies in English Literature* 9 (Spring 1969): 283–301.

Curtis, Harry, Jr. "The Year Growing Ancient: Formal Ambiguity in *The Winter's Tale*." *CLA Journal* 23 (June 1980): 431–37.

Cutts, John P. *Rich and Strange: A Study of Shakespeare's Last Plays*. Pullman: Washington State University Press, 1968.

Dash, Irene G. "A Penchant for Perdita on the Eighteenth-Century English Stage." *Studies in Eighteenth Century Culture* 6 (1977): 331–46.

Edwards, Philip. "Shakespeare's Romances: 1900–57." *Shakespeare Survey* 11 (1958): 1–18.

Ewbank, Inga-Stina. "The Triumph of Time in *The Winter's Tale*." *Review of English Literature* 5 (1964): 83–100.

Fox, G. P. *The Winter's Tale*. Oxford: Basil Blackwell, 1967.

Frey, Charles. *Shakespeare's Vast Romance: A Study of* The Winter's Tale. Columbia: University of Missouri Press, 1980.

Frye, Northrop. *Anatomy of Criticism*. Princeton: Princeton University Press, 1957.

———. "The Argument of Comedy." In *English Institute Essays* (1948), edited by D. A. Robertson, 58–73. New York: Columbia University Press, 1949.

————. *A Natural Perspective: The Development of Shakespearean Comedy and Romance*. New York: Columbia University Press, 1955. Reprint. New York: Harcourt, Brace & World, 1965.

————. "Recognition in *The Winter's Tale*." In *Essays on Shakespeare and Elizabethan Drama*, edited by Richard Horley. Columbia: University of Missouri Press, 1962. Reprinted in Frye's *Fables of Identity*. New York: Harcourt, Brace & World, 1963.

Garber, Marjorie. "Coming of Age in Shakespeare." *Yale Review* 66 (1977): 517–33.

Goddard, Harold C. *The Meaning of Shakespeare*. Chicago: University of Chicago Press, 1951.

Greenlaw, E. "Shakespeare's Pastorals." *Studies in Philology* 13 (1916): 122–54.

Gurr, Andrew. "The Bear, the Statue and Hysteria in *The Winter's Tale*." *Shakespeare Quarterly* 34 (Winter 1983): 420–25.

Hoeniger, F. D. "The Meaning of *The Winter's Tale*." *University of Toronto Quarterly* 20 (1950): 11–26.

James, D. G. *Scepticism and Poetry*. New York: Barnes & Noble, 1960.

Jones, Emrys. *The Origins of Shakespeare*. London: Oxford University Press, 1977.

Kermode, Frank. *William Shakespeare: The Final Plays*. London: Longmans, Green, 1963.

Knight, G. Wilson. *The Crown of Life*. London: Methuen, 1958.

————. *The Shakespearean Tempest*. London: Oxford University Press, 1932. Reprint. London: Methuen, 1971.

Krier, Theresa M. "The Triumph of Time: Paradox in *The Winter's Tale*." *Centennial Review* 26 (1982): 341–53.

Lawlor, John. "*Pandosto* and the Nature of Dramatic Romance." *Philological Quarterly* 41 (1962): 96–113.

Leavis, F. R. "Criticism of Shakespeare's Last Plays." *Scrutiny* 10 (1942): 339–45. Reprinted in *The Common Pursuit*. London: Chatto & Windus, 1952; Penguin, 1962.

Mahood, M. M. *Shakespeare's Wordplay*. London: Methuen, 1957.

Matchett, William. "Some Dramatic Techniques in *The Winter's Tale*." *Shakespeare Survey* 22 (1971): 93–107.

McDonald, Russ. "Poetry and Plot in *The Winter's Tale*." *Shakespeare Quarterly* 36, no. 3 (1985): 315–29.

Mowat, Barbara A. *The Dramaturgy of Shakespeare's Romances*. Athens: University of Georgia Press, 1976.

Muir, Kenneth. *Shakespeare: The Winter's Tale: A Casebook*. London: Macmillan, 1968.

Nuttal, William. *William Shakespeare: The Winter's Tale*. London: Edward Arnold, 1966.

Peterson, Douglas L. *Time, Tide and Tempest*. San Marino, Calif.: Huntington Library, 1973.

Pettet, E. C. *Shakespeare and the Romance Tradition*. London and New York: Staples Press, 1949. Reprint. London: Methuen, 1970.

Proudfoot, Richard. "Verbal Reminiscence and the Two–Part Structure of *The Winter's Tale*." *Shakespeare Survey* 29 (1976): 67–78.

Pyle, Fitzroy. The Winter's Tale: *A Commentary on the Structure*. London: Routledge & Kegan Paul, 1969.

Schanzer, Ernest. "The Structural Pattern of *The Winter's Tale*." *Review of English Literature* 5 (1964): 72–82.

Schwartz, Murray. "*The Winter's Tale:* Loss and Transformation." *American Imago* 32 (1975): 145–99.

Smith, Jonathan. "The Language of Leontes." *Shakespeare Quarterly* 19 (1968): 317–22.

Spencer, Theodore. "Appearance and Reality in Shakespeare's Last Plays." *Modern Philology* 39 (1942): 265–74.

Strachey, Lytton. "Shakespeare's Final Period." In *Books and Characters*. London: Chatto & Windus; New York: Harcourt, Brace, 1949.

Taylor, Michael. "Innocence in *The Winter's Tale*." *Shakespeare Studies* 15 (1982): 227–42.

Tillyard, E. M. W. *Shakespeare's Last Plays*. London: Chatto & Windus, 1938. Reprint, 1964.

Traversi, Derek. *Shakespeare: The Last Phase*. London: Hollis & Carter, 1954.

Weinstein, Philip M. "An Interpretation of Pastoral in *The Winter's Tale*." *Shakespeare Quarterly* 22 (1971): 97–109.

Young, David. *The Heart's Forest: A Study of Shakespeare's Pastoral Plays*. New Haven: Yale University Press, 1972.

Acknowledgments

" 'Great Creating Nature': An Essay on *The Winter's Tale*" by G. Wilson Knight from *The Crown of Life: Essays in Interpretation of Shakespeare's Final Plays* by G. Wilson Knight, © 1958 by Methuen & Co. Ltd. Reprinted by permission.

" 'But It Appears She Lives': Iteration in *The Winter's Tale*" by James Edward Siemon from *PMLA* 89, no. 1 (January 1974), © 1974 by the Modern Language Association of America. Reprinted by permission.

" 'Integration' in *The Winter's Tale*" by L. C. Knights from *The Sewanee Review* 84 (Fall 1976), © 1976 by the University of the South. Reprinted by permission of the editor.

"Women and Issue in *The Winter's Tale*" by Carol Thomas Neely from *Philological Quarterly* 57, no. 2 (Spring 1978), © 1978 by the University of Iowa. Reprinted by permission.

"Tragic Structure in *The Winter's Tale*: The Affective Dimension" by Charles Frey from *Shakespeare's Romances Reconsidered*, edited by Carol McGinnis Kay and Henry E. Jacobs, © 1978 by the University of Nebraska Press. Reprinted by permission.

"Leontes and the Spider: Language and Speaker in Shakespeare's Last Plays" by Anne Barton from *Shakespeare's Styles: Essays in Honour of Kenneth Muir*, edited by Philip Edwards, Inga-Stina Ewbank, and G. K. Hunter, © 1980 by Cambridge University Press. Reprinted by permission.

"Shakespeare's Humanist Enterprise: *The Winter's Tale*" by Louis L. Martz from *English Renaissance Studies: Presented to Dame Helen Gardner in Honour of Her Seventieth Birthday* by Louis L. Martz, © 1980 by Oxford University Press. Reprinted by permission.

"Shakespeare's Bohemia Revisited: A Caveat" by Richard Studing from *Shakespeare Studies: An Annual Gathering of Research, Criticism and Reviews* 15, edited by J. Leeds Barroll III, © 1982 by the Council for Research in the Renaissance. Reprinted by permission.

Index

legend and fairy-tale, 121;
art-nature theme in, 35–36,
38–39, 40–41, 43–45, 48, 49,
119, 145–46; Autolycus's role in,
120, 133–34, 143–44, 145;
beginning of, 102–3; birth and
breeding imagery in, 78–79;
Camillo's role in, 52–53; Christian
overtones of, 20–22, 26–27,
28, 30–31, 36–37, 42–43, 45, 73,
130–31, 136–37; as comedy, 1,
29–30, 47, 53, 89, 121;
complicated plot of, 52; conflict
of the soul in, 63–64, 73–74; as
corrupted pastoral, 141–49;
death in, 19, 44, 94–96; dreams
in, 56; dualities and antitheses
in, 117, 118; eternity in, 37–38,
41, 44; evil in, 14–16, 18, 27;
false fictions in, 118–21; father-
daughter reunion in, 34;
generative counterplot of non-
Leontean scenes of, 96–97;
good versus evil in, 47–48,
57–58; Greek aspects of nature
in, 22–25, 28; Greek mythology
in, 57, 69, 81, 135–36; Greek
names for characters of, 123–24;
Greek tragedy compared with,
126–27, 130–31; Hermione's
death in, 26, 28–29, 36, 54–57;
Hermione's resurrection in, 7, 22,
31–33, 34–43, 50, 51–52,
72–73, 85–87, 120, 121, 138;
Hermione's trial in, 23–25; 67,
69, 118; integration in, 63–64, 70,
73–74; irony in, 106; iterative
structure of, 47–48, 57–58; as
"Leonteia," 131; Leontes and
"nothingness" in, 2, 13–14, 45;
Leontes' association with exits
and goings in, 91–93; Leontes'
jealousy in, 2–3, 10–12, 17, 26,
27, 47, 49–50, 53, 65, 67, 68,
76–77, 90, 91, 127–30; Leontes'

newborn daughter in, 17, 19, 20,
21, 33, 67, 92; love between
Perdita and Florizel in, 3–4, 47,
51, 68, 70, 83–84, 147, 148;
lower-class characters in, 112;
Mamillius's role in, 11;
masculine world of, 76–78;
misogyny in, 91, 93–95, 98,
148; nature in, 18, 19–20, 19–24,
28, 38, 43–45, 68–69, 73, 132,
134–36; originality of, 4–5;
pastoral conventions in, 1, 4,
67–69, 131–36, 139–40; pastoral
as mirror of Leontes' passion in,
140–49; Paulina's role in, 16,
18–19, 26–27, 30–31, 40, 44,
81–82, 99, 137; penitence in,
26–27; Perdita's nature in, 1–2,
3–4, 32–33, 50, 65–66,
68–69, 83; Perdita's return in,
34, 44, 71–72; as romance, 1,
7, 47, 87–88, 99; season imagery
in, 8, 26; sexual issues in,
53–54, 87; source of plot of,
63; speech in, 12–13, 14, 64–66,
107, 111; spider story of Leontes
in, 103–4, 115–16, 118–19;
statue scene in, 34, 35–36,
38–39, 55, 131; summer festival
in, 134–36, 144–48; themes
of, 8, 43–45, 50–52, 58,
85–87; three-part action of,
8, 131; time in, 37–38, 44;
tyranny in, 16–17, 19, 21,
23, 24–26, 43–44, 140, 143,
148–49; women in, 75–88;
youth versus maturity in, 8–10,
19–20, 22, 33, 38, 71, 84. *See also
individual characters*
Witch of Atlas, The (Shelley),
42
Wordsworth, William, 22, 23, 45

Yeats, William Butler, 41, 62